An American Family

Gerald H Frieling Jr.

ISBN: 1500559172
ISBN 13: 9781500559175

To all those family members, past and present,
who have contributed to the richness of this story.

Table of Contents

Foreword

This book is about an American family, my family, which is not much different than all the other immigrant families that came to America seeking a better life and greater opportunity. It is the story of various families coming together much like tributaries flowing into an ever-widening river. The stories, experiences, and heartaches that fill the pages are rich with history and values that develop into the fabric of the family culture.

My mother, Mary Ann Coons Frieling, always asked whether the children and grandchildren had learned and retained the family's values. To be able to answer that question, I had first to define what those values were. As both the values within the family and the culture at large have evolved over time, this book attempts to go back to the beginnings of our family and trace the evolution of those values. Our family's values were influenced by new members joining the family and new generations coming on to the scene as well as by the changing influences, attitudes, and mores of society in general.

The purpose of *An American Family* is to stimulate thoughtful reflection and discussion by the current and future members of the family with the hope that they will continue to build upon the family's legacy. Through the examination of our family's history, hopefully, certain patterns will emerge that shed light on our family's shared values, such as the high priority placed on continued education, the prominence of quality long-term marriages, and the importance of generosity towards those less fortunate. Today we are dealing with difficult and contentious issues on a national level. The story of *An American Family* provides guidance to make rational decisions on issues by teaching the positive fundamentals of culture. Decisions should not be made on important issues on the basis of short-term emotions, the influence of social media or the views of 24-hour talk shows. Hopefully, this foundation will provide the basis to make good and reasoned decisions on current issues and further enhance the family's values and cultural fundamentals.

While the reader will find both humorous and engaging passages, the objective is for succeeding generations not only to learn of our family's story, but also to embrace the struggles, the successes, and the values, that will lead to a fuller and richer life. Further, I hope that the grandchildren and others who may read the book will be inspired by our family's journey. Hopefully, they will teach their children to preserve the family's values and continue the family story.

Introduction

The occasion for writing this book is a celebration – the celebration of Mary Ann Coons Frieling, my mother on her 108th birthday. In conversations with my mother over the years she always asked if the children had learned the cultural values of the family. I never knew quite how to answer that question because first, I wasn't sure what were the full range of values she was talking about and second, I was pretty sure our family's values have been shaped over time, subject to the various life situations and even personalities of our family members.

A recent book by Malcolm Gladwell, *Outliers: The Story of Success*, gets to the heart of mother's question. (It is apropos that the book is largely about success in education as success in education has been central to our family's legacy for over a century.) Gladwell attempts to account for the various factors in my initial hesitancy to answer my mother's question: "heritage, opportunity, accident and maybe genes after all". According to Gladwell, there is another factor, which he calls "cultural legacy."

Sociologists classify cultural legacies under "intangible cultural heritage," a subset of the larger "cultural heritage." These intangibles consist of non-physical aspects of a particular society or family, often maintained by social customs during a specific period in history. These include social values and traditions, customs and practices, aesthetic and spiritual beliefs, artistic expression, language and other aspects of human activity. Gladwell continues: "Cultural legacies are powerful forces. They have deep roots and long lives. They persist, generation after generation, virtually intact, even as the economic and social and demographic conditions that spawned them have vanished, and they play such a role in directing attitudes and behavior that we cannot make sense of our world without them."

These academic definitions of "cultural legacies" and "intangible cultural heritage" are very similar to what my mother called the family's cultural values. Cultural values are central to a family and it is families like ours that create, maintain and modify those values as they are passed from one generation to the next. And central to our family's values are the experiences and values of my mother, both as the sum of those who came before her and as inspiration to those of us who came after. Because her story is so important to the family's story, I refer to her as Mother throughout this book. Mother wanted the family to know how her experiences and values influenced her life and actions in the hope that the family's cultural values will continue to shape generations to come.

Everyone who has listened to Mother tell the family stories has come away with the same thought – that we should preserve them for future generations. The story of our family is similar in some aspects to many of other families whose ancestors immigrated to America in hopes of finding a better life and fulfilling what has been called the "American Dream," hence the title of the book. There are also many unique and interesting elements to our story, sometimes even at the center of our country's story, as some in our family, for example, played important roles in the Revolutionary and Civil wars.

With the help of many family members, some close and others distant, I will try to recreate their journeys to the extent that our research will permit. To the extent that I am able, I will address the cultural values that arose from the particular historical situation of the family and were maintained and modified over time. The outline of the book will be to take each direct branch of the family and trace its origin as far back as I have information. I will obviously not be able to trace all of the brothers, sisters, cousins, second marriages, in-laws, etc. I will sometimes depart from the direct line to include interesting stories that will add richness to the story and shed light on our family's cultural values. I hope you will find our American family's journey interesting and enlightening and perhaps also, as an inspiration for future generations.

Mary Ann (Coons) Frieling

CHAPTER 1

Early years – The Frieling Family

The Frieling name took its initial formation between the 11th and 13th centuries and was first recorded as a descriptive identification to distinguish one person from another. By 1490 the root name, Friedl, had become a recognized surname and was passed on to others in the family.

The Crusades began in the year 1095 under the direction of Pope Urban II at the time when our name was evolving. The Crusades created a need for identifying names and symbols. These took the form of coats-of-arms such as is represented on the cover of this book. Heralds recorded these armorial bearings and it is from these records that we have the confirmed coat-of-arms for our family with the motto from the German language of "Honesty-Hard Work-Generosity". The specific shape of the shield dates back to the 13th century. Its function then was to ward off arrows shot from crossbows and protection from battle-axes and swords.

Prior to 1500 the family lived in Germany, probably in the Hanover area, moving to Almelo, Holland about the time of Martin Luther's protestant reformation 1522-1546. During this tumultuous time, our family made decisions whose impact is still felt today. During the reformation a part of the family, as the story goes, "changed the spelling of their name remained Roman Catholic and moved 10 miles down the road". Our branch of the family became protestant and remained in Almelo but later moved to Groningen, Netherlands, where my great grandfather, Theophilus was born in 1836 to Tones Frieling and his wife (unknown).

When I was employed at Texas Instruments in Attleboro, MA: 1959-1969, I had the opportunity on occasion to visit our plant in Bedford,

England. Bedford is a mid-size town located about 50 miles north of London and it is of great importance when tracing my Mother's family, but TI also had a plant located in Almelo, Holland. The manager of that facility had married a Frieling. She had done some major research on the origin of the Frieling family and I rely upon her for the early history of our family. Unfortunately the church where many of the records were stored burned in the early 1960's and I was unable to obtain any written confirmation of her story.

By the time Theophilus turned 21 in 1857, The Netherlands was in turmoil. After Napoleon's defeat at Waterloo in 1815 The Congress of Vienna remapped Europe uniting Belgium and Holland under a Dutch King but the political, social and economic customs were so different between the two countries that in 1830 Belgium revolted and declared its independence. The Dutch were also about to lose Luxembourg. At the same time Prussia chose Otto von Bismarck as prime minister with the objective of unifying Germany. Groningen is directly across the border from Prussia, and although Theophilus and his family continued to attend church in Groningen they went to school and were educated in Prussia. During that period more students learned to read and write but the schools were designed to make the people better soldiers and indeed in 1864 Prussia seized the Dutch provinces of Schleswig and Holstein. It was in this environment that as a young man Theophilus decided to immigrate to America.

He arrived in Chicago, IL and soon married Geerzina (Gezina) Harka Bolhuis. As Geerzina was also from Groningen, Municipality: Middlesturn, Netherlands, It is probable that they knew each other before arriving in America. My Grandfather, Thomas, was born in Chicago on August 20, 1870.

The Great Chicago Fire occurred in 1871 wiping out the central business district, destroying over 17,000 buildings, killing at least 300 people and leaving 90,000 homeless. Though the exact family situation is uncertain, Theophilus and his family were surely affected. When

Thomas was 6 years of age and his brother Harke was 4, they moved to Grand Rapids, Michigan integrating into the Dutch community there.

In total, Theophilus and Geerzina had seven children – all boys. Five died in infancy. Only Thomas and Harke survived. Harke went to Calvin College, near where they lived, and then attended Hope College seminary in Holland, Michigan becoming a pastor in the Dutch Reformed Church. He served churches in Grand Rapids, Michigan; Fulton, Illinois; LaFayette, Indiana and Paterson, New Jersey where he died at age 76.

Thomas grew up in Grand Rapids where he met his future wife, Kaatje (Katherine or Kate) Glupker. She was the daughter of Johannus (John) Glupker and Andina (Dina) Broene. They were farmers from Hanover (Hohenkorben in the county of Bentheim), Germany immigrating to this country after the Civil War in 1865. Andina immigrated with her father and siblings two months later. They were from Hocklenkamp, Germany (also in the Hanover region). Two of her brothers, Egbert and Geert were both Dutch Reform ministers and settled in Fillmore Township, Allegan County, Michigan. John and Dina were married on March 28, 1867 in Laketown (East Saugatuck) Michigan. John died there in 1922. Dina passed away in 1870, 6 months after Kate was born. On July 14, 1880 John married Alberdina Hermanna Doren in Grand Rapids, Michigan. Alberdina was 29 years of age at the time of the marriage.

Thomas's brother Harke married Thomas and Katherine on June 29, 1899 in Three Oaks, Berrien County, Michigan. They had four children; Grace born March 29, 1900, Gerald Harvey, my father, born January 28, 1903, Arthur John born September 26, 1908 and Theodore Franklin born June 26, 1910.

The first of Thomas and Katherine's children, Grace, was a large woman with a heart of gold. She had several boy friends during her life but chose not to marry and lived with her parents until their death. Thomas died from a stroke on September 13, 1949 after a long career

3

with the Grand Rapids Press. He worked his way up from a typesetter to the Press Room. He was a kind and gentle man who loved to walk to the bakery in the morning. When I was there in the summers I would walk with him to the bakery and we would have great discussions. When we went to the cottage in Grand Haven, Michigan we would often go fishing together for perch off the pier.

I have wonderful memories of Grandfather Frieling. Kate, on the other hand was very strong-willed with definite ideas about life and tough as nails. I remember one Saturday Grace and Kate asked me to go to their favorite restaurant for dinner. I dressed in my best shirt and pants. Kate took one look and said, "Is that the best you have?" and then promptly changed the reservations to another restaurant. A take-away from that experience is that appearance matters. A good rule of thumb is that you should always dress as good or better for either a social or professional occasion than the best dressed person in the room. When Kate went to California to visit her son Art, she fell and broke her leg. In the hospital there were only certain select people she would allow in the room to attend to her. She was one tough and stubborn lady. Kate died November 7, 1961.

Grace continued to live in the house until her death on January 9, 1968. In her will she stipulated that Art was to receive an extra $1,000 because after Kate died he told her that whatever happened she would always have a home with him and his wife Hazel. Grace never forgot that act of kindness. During her working years she was employed by the Michigan Consolidated Gas Company where she enjoyed a deserved reputation for knowledge and teamwork.

My father, Gerald (Jerry or Jed), was the first person in the family to attend college. He went to the University of Michigan where he studied Civil Engineering and played two years of varsity basketball. In the summers he worked as the supervisor of Garfield Park, which was a large city owned facility near their home. He graduated in 1926, received a job offer from the Kansas City Public Service Company, and relocated to Kansas City. In Kansas City he met my Mother, Mary Ann Coons, on a blind date and married her on July 31, 1928 in Excelsior Springs, Missouri.

While my father was serious and responsible, Arthur was somewhat of a free spirit. It was often said in our family that he would have been perfect for the role of Nathan Detroit in the musical "Guys and Dolls". He married Hazel Brastrom on July 28, 1936. Until the outbreak of World War II he worked as a home appliance salesman for Michigan Gas. After the war he became the sales manager for a California-based chemical company and moved his family there. They had three children: Larry born December 19, 1939 who became a very accomplished aeronautical engineer, Carole born June 7, 1944, a favorite of Grace, and Barbara born June 13, 1947. Barbara was beautiful and often compared to a "Barbie Doll," but unfortunately, she had a severe hearing problem that could never be corrected. Hazel had a long career with the United States Postal Service passing away on July 4, 1989. Art passed away on October 28, 1998 in Hemet, California.

Ted, the last of Thomas and Kate's children was a handsome man who seemed to have an endless supply of girl friends. He married Olivia (Ollie) Secord on August 5, 1939, whose father was a Vice President of the Hudson Motor Car Company. The wedding was in Grosse Pointe, Michigan, with the reception at the Grosse Pointe Country Club. It was a memorable event made more so when Ollie's veil caught on fire from one of the candles. She was not injured but it caused a lot of excitement and was a point of recollection in our family for years.

Ted was a Lieutenant Commander in the U.S. Navy during World War II serving most of the time at the Bureau of Personnel where he rewrote the manual for the disposition and transfer of Navy Personnel throughout the world. After the war Ted was in the oil distribution business. Ollie graduated from Eastern Michigan University and was a very accomplished woman. She was employed in the Detroit school system as a woodworking and general manual trades teacher. She wrote a textbook on the subject, which became the standard for the school system. For our wedding she made us a terrific white mahogany coffee table. Ted died November 27, 1992 of congestive heart failure and Ollie in 1995 of cancer of the lymph nodes.

Ted and Olivia had one son, Thomas Bertram, born on July 23, 1943, who became an airline captain first for TWA and then Continental Airlines. Thomas has one son, William Theodore, by his first wife. Tom, Bill, together with his family, and Tom's second wife, Mary Ann, all live in Evergreen, Colorado.

My experiences with my grandparents and their children were often centered at the summerhouse they all shared in Grand Haven, Michigan. The rented the same large six-bedroom house on the Dunes of Lake Michigan. Even though they all led busy and successful lives, all four of my grandparents' children, along with their spouses, were always there. Since I am the oldest grandchild of Thomas and Katherine by ten years, I was often the lone child milling about the lake house with Aunt Grace, my parents, Uncle Arthur (and later, Aunt Hazel), and Uncle Ted (and later, Aunt Ollie). Although this shared emphasis on the importance of family has always been a family legacy, the practical implementation of this time cannot be overstated. Because of the closeness of the family, suitors and potential spouses had to earn acceptance from the other siblings, and especially from Grandmother Kate, whose personality has never been described as "warm and fuzzy". My mother, being a farm girl from Missouri, had a particularly difficult time earning her acceptance.

Thomas & Kate Frieling

Ted, Art, Thomas, Jerry, & Jerry, Sr. Frieling at the beach in Grand Haven, MI - 1933

Gerald H. Frieling – Graduation at
the University of Michigan, 1926

Mary Ann, Casey, Jerry, Lori, Sarah, Bob,
Carly, Nancy, Anne, Leigh & Grant
GrandDad's Birthday - 1995

CHAPTER 2

Early years – The Odell Family

The story of Mother's side of the family is rich with history and I am deeply indebted to my second cousin, twice removed, Derrell Hankins of Kansas City, Missouri and his associates for the remarkable research they have performed. The Odell family can be traced to Walter I, Castellan of Lens and Cambrai in Flanders 972-979. He was descended from the Count of Lens. His son Walter II married Ermentrude and their daughter and heiress, Adela, married Hugh d'Oisy, Castellan of Douai. Their son Walter De Flanders invaded Saxon England with William the Conqueror in 1066 and was granted the barony of Wahull in Bedfordshire and Northamptonshire for his service becoming the first Baron de Wahull. Walter was, in fact, the younger son and in those days that meant not having much of a future of his own which is probably why he joined forces with William. They were fortunate on the timing of the invasion as the King of England had to divide his forces to repel both an attack from the North by the Scots and William from the South.

It is because the family was titled and Walter held a barony in two counties that the family is so well documented. According to the Domesday, Book Walter held 5,625 acres of land in Bedfordshire and 6,705 acres in Northamptonshire making his total holdings 12,330 acres including all villages, livestock, farming equipment, buildings, people and some slaves. His castle was built northwest of Bedford. The same Bedford mentioned earlier when discussing the Frieling history. There is nothing left of the castle or the barony today although it is mentioned several times in the history of the area. However, there is a town of Odell near its former location. Over time, the family name changed spelling from Wahul to Wahull to Wahulle to Woodhulle to Woodhull. In the English vernacular, Woodhull was pronounced ODLE giving rise to the name Odell.

Through the years there were 19 Baron de Woodhull (Odell). The Barony of Odell went dormant in 1542 when the estates passed to Agnes Woodhull and no longer exists. It was common by 1542 that lands passed to the eldest daughter if there were no older male heirs but the title did not pass to her son. He researched the Barony and laid claim to the title during the reign of James I. The claim was authenticated and pronounced valid but James did not sign it. He didn't deny it; he just didn't act on it. The most likely reason being that seniority in the House of Lords is based on the age of the title and this title would have been among the oldest - making him senior to almost everybody. The King's move was very political because there could be no appeal, and by not acting on it lots of powerful people were made happy. No doubt this was one of the reasons the family decided to take their farming and land management skills to America.

The next in line was William Woodhull (Odell) who was born about 1600. He married Rebecca Brown and came to America with her and their sons, John and William II, before 1639. They settled first in Concord, Massachusetts Bay Colony, and then later moved to Fairfield, Connecticut where a grant of land was recorded on April 8, 1660. William died in Fairfield and his will was entered on June 6, 1676. In total they had five children. William II was born in 1634, married Sarah Vowles, daughter of William Vowles. William II died in 1697. He and Sarah had eight children. One son, Isaac Odell, born 1676 married Anne Tompkins. Isaac and Anne had seven children including another Isaac born 1696. This Isaac married Sarah Hoyt and they had four children including another Isaac who was born in 1750. He served in the Revolutionary War as a guide for the Continental Army.

He married Abigail Mansfield and died on February 14, 1834 in Ray County, Missouri.

William II had another son, John, born in Fairfield, CT and was awarded land grants by the General Assembly of the town of Fairfield. One of his sons was the Honorable and Reverend Johnathan Odell, a noted loyalist. He was a medical doctor who graduated from the College of New Jersey (now Princeton University) and served as a surgeon in the British Army. When the infamous Major John Andre (he was later hanged for treason) was captured during the Revolutionary War, he was carrying papers that laid out the plans of Benedict Arnold to surrender West Point.

Those letters were from our cousin Rev. Johnathan Odell. After the incident, he fled for his life to New Brunswick, Canada, and after the revolution made claims for the property he lost when he went to Canada.

The story of Benedict Arnold does provide an illustration on how we can have two reputations and not just one. Arnold was a hero of the Revolutionary War, survived a life-threatening wound at the Battle of Saratoga and became one of the Continental Army's top generals and thereby earned a reputation for being highly competent. However, when he defected to the British his character was questioned and his name has become a byword for treachery.

Rev. Johnathan had a son John born in 1756 and was a cousin to General Jacob Odell. John was a staunch patriot and Colonel of a regiment of the Westchester County Militia. In 1776, John was left almost destitute by the British encamping on his farm and destroying his property. From 1780 to the end of the war he did remarkable work for the patriot cause, and was so well known and feared by the British that they offered a reward of 100 pounds for his capture. He was the principal guide in the advance of the continental army through the

Saw Mill or Nepperham River Valley on July 2 & 3, 1781. A memorial was dedicated to him by the State legislature of New York in 1839 that set forth his public services.

Isaac and Abigail also had a son named Isaac, now the third one in three generations. This Isaac was born September 29, 1778 and began the family's migration to the West. Like many families during this period the migration went through Pennsylvania, down the Ohio River to Kentucky and then through the Cumberland Gap to Tennessee. Isaac met and married Nancy Hutchins in the early 1800's in Cocke County, Tennessee. In the early days Cocke County became the "Mother" of Ray County, Missouri, which was organized in 1821, the same year the state of Missouri was taken from the Territory of Missouri. The Odell family was a large part of the contingent of families that moved from East Tennessee. Between 1818 & 1819 the Odell's and a German family, the Tarwater's migrated from Eastern Tennessee to Western Ray County. Nancy was born in 1787 and died on May 26, 1855. Isaac died on January 29, 1855. The couple had 11 or more children one of which, William Odell, was born on December 9, 1805. He married Mary Odell (no relation) a daughter of John Odell, on January 29, 1832, in Ray County, Missouri. Mary was born in 1816 and had 12 children with William. She died in 1903. William died March 22, 1865, just a month before the end of the Civil War.

Andrew Jackson Odell was born to Isaac and Nancy in 1833. He was first married to Elizabeth Whitten on September 16, 1857 in Ray County, Missouri. They had two children, Mary Jane and George. Andrew (Jack) enrolled as a sergeant in the Confederate Army on January 11, 1862, at Richmond, Missouri. He served with the 3rd Regiment of the Missouri State Militia volunteers, which was later consolidated with Company "B" on February 4, 1863. They fought in many battles in southwest Missouri and northwest Arkansas. Missouri ranks third among the states in Civil War battles behind only Virginia and

Tennessee. Elizabeth died later in 1863. Andrew (Jack) came home to take care of the children after the expiration of his three-year term of service (but before the end of the war) in February 1865. Between 1863 and 1865 Mary Jane lived with her Grandparents William and Mary Odell. She was four years of age.

On April 2, 1865, Andrew (Jack) married Mahala Woods, only a few months after he had been discharged from the Confederate Army. He moved the family to a 160-acre farm he bought 3 miles southeast of Excelsior Springs, Missouri, on the Clay-Ray county line. Mary Jane then began attending subscription school in the old Jasper church. Her father notched trees so she could find her way to and from school in the heavily wooded hills. Andrew died when she was nearing her 14th birthday and again Mary Jane went to live with her Grandmother. Her Grandfather died March 22, 1865 about 10 days before her father remarried.

Joseph N. Carothers of Milan, Sullivan County, Missouri, had rented about 60 acres of Andrew Jackson Odell's farm. He, of course, knew and the courted Mary Jane. They were married on October 14, 1877, when she was 17 years of age. They became the parents of four children: Chloe May, my Grandmother, William Jackson, Ralph and Joseph, Jr. In 1886 Joe Carothers was working in the field when he had an attack of appendicitis. He suffered for three days, and since medical assistance was not available, he died. Mary Jane and her four children continued to live in the old log house that was on the farm when they bought it from her stepmother, Mahala, in 1876.

Two years after her husband's death, Mary Jane contracted for the erection of a new home that she and Joe had planned before his unexpected death. The supervisors and workers were all from the local area and excellent craftsmen. The house had two wells for drinking water and a cistern to catch rainwater outside with a water pump in the kitchen for general use. There was a two-hole outhouse behind the house, a large oak tree in the front yard and space on the side for a large garden.

Despite being a widow at 27, Mary Jane not only managed and built the family home she also became a successful businesswoman. Her chief income was from dairy products and the sale of timber. A practical problem that had to be overcome was how to get the dairy products to market. In the past they just rode their horses over the fields but this was not sufficient for transporting any quantity of goods. The solution was to build a road. So Mary Jane donated a portion of her property and convinced others to do likewise. All the neighbors pitched in and built the road, which is still in use today.

Mary Jane was resourceful, self-reliant, and well respected in the community. She never remarried. She planted cotton, combed it, weaved it into cloth, and sewed it for the children's clothes. She also sheered the sheep, processing the wool for blankets and other articles of clothing. It was not unusual for her to can 200 quarts of fruit, vegetables, and sausage to last over the cold winter months. An article, which appeared in the Excelsior Springs Daily Standard, described her "as an outstanding person whose thrift, patience and strong work ethic established a home that is an example of excellent management".

The house that Mary Jane built and the property on which it stands played a significant role in our family history, both as a literal place and a representative of the importance of "home." The property that Andrew purchased was originally a land sale by the United States Government. It was executed on September 7, 1838, and signed by President Martin Van Buren. At that time there was also a tribe of the Osage Indians living on the West side near the stream. Over the years, Mary Jane became friends with two of the Indian ladies. When the Indians were forced to move to the reservation in Oklahoma they gave her two flowering bushes that they had been cultivating. Mary Jane planted them at the front entrance to the farm and I can remember admiring them and her taking great pride in telling me the story. The Indians also provided me a great collection of arrow and spearheads. Before he purchased a tractor, Ralph plowed the fields with two mules. I used to walk behind the plows and pick up these Indian relics from the plowed ground.

On the North side of the property ran the Butterfield Stage line. It did not go into Kansas at all because the Union controlled that territory. It ran south from the Missouri River to Fort Smith, Arkansas. Confederate General Sterling Price used this road repeatedly. From Fort Smith it went into Oklahoma and then on to Texas. The route started in 1858 but was taken over completely by the Confederate military in 1862. There were two other Butterfield Stage routes established; one in 1858 transporting both mail and passengers from St. Louis to Tipton, Missouri to San Francisco, California and a freight route from Atchison, Kansas to Denver, Colorado.

The overland route to California took 24 days. The first passenger described it as "24 days of hell" but it was shorter and took less time than a ship going around Cape Horn. A typical breakfast on the trail consisted of being served on the bottom of a candle box with the passengers sitting on upside down pails. No plates were available, only tin cups for coffee and no milk or sugar. Short bread was baked over coals with the men buttering it with their pocketknives and being reminded to hurry so the chickens would not eat it.

The freight route was called the Smoky Hill Trail and was prompted by the discovery of gold near Denver. The stage was the quickest route there. It ran for about 600 miles with relay stations built every twelve miles for the passenger's comfort. It ran from June 1865 to August 1870. As the Kansas Pacific Railroad moved closer to Denver the stage line was no longer needed and that marked the end of the stagecoach era in American history. The Pony Express also shared a station near the farm property with the stagecoach. I had two letters that had been carried by the Pony Express that I used in a Show and Tell session at grade school.

Also on the road past the farm going north toward Excelsior Springs is a monument to the Civil War Battle of Fredericksburg, Missouri. Union soldiers that were part of the 2nd Colorado Cavalry were on patrol from their post in Liberty, Missouri, looking for Confederate guerrillas. There was first a skirmish on July 14, 1864, then a battle on July 17th. Six Union soldiers were killed with 4 wounded and 2 missing. Those killed are buried in the old Pisgah Cemetery. The wounded were brought up to the Baptist church in the area that was founded and built by a relative of Sidney Coons wife. The church was used as both a hospital and morgue. Another battle took place in the same area on August 12th with 4 killed or wounded.

Although the property is full of important American history, the real story is the perseverance and strength of character of Mary Jane. If we are defined not by our circumstances, but by the choices we make in light of these circumstances, Mary Jane was the living definition of a strong woman. Her father left for the Civil War when she was 4 years of age entrusting her care to his parents. When Andrew Jackson (Jack) returned from the war three years later, he remarried within 6 months. Further, Jack and Mahala soon had a child together. Then Jack died when she was 13 years of age and Mary Jane again went to live with her grandmother; her grandfather had died in 1865. It is no wonder that she married Joe Carothers when she was 17. Unfortunately they only had about nine years together before he died leaving her a widow at age 27 with three young children. The fourth child, Joseph, Jr., was born four months after his dad died. All of them lived in a small log cabin.

Similar to the Frieling summerhouse on Lake Michigan, the importance to our family of Mary Jane and the house she managed to build cannot be overstated. Not only was it a beautiful home with a wide variety of flowers, roses, and shrubbery, it was also a loving home in the fullest sense of the word. It would provide both physical and emotional refuge for generations to come. As an illustration, in the late 1950's and early 60's when sons John and Bob were young, we would drive the road from the highway to the farm, which because of its roller coaster character was called the Wee road. It was a lot of fun to drive and a thrill for the boys until one day we were driving the Bigham Cadillac hit a bump and ripped the exhaust system from under the car. John and Bob also had great memories of having the best biscuits in the world off the old wood stove, watching Ralph milk the cows and helping the grandmothers shell new peas. Lasting memories that again made the farm a special place.

Farmhouse at Excelsior Springs, MO

Butterfield Stagecoach

Andrew Jackson Odell in his Confederate Army Uniform 1862

Chloe May, Berenice, Julie, Robert Sidney, Mary Jane,
Mary Ann, Jerry, Mary Jo
A Family Christmas

CHAPTER 3

Early years – The Coons Family

As mentioned in the previous chapter, the strength of character exhibited by my great grandmother, Mary Jane, in the most difficult of personal circumstances left a lasting legacy in our family. On October 3, 1878, Mary Jane and Joseph Carothers gave birth to the oldest of their four children, Chloe May, in their small log cabin. Joseph would pass away in 1886, leaving her without a father at age seven. Even at that young age, she had no choice but to become a primary caregiver to her three brothers. Chloe May was an attractive girl and attended the local country school by riding her pony across the undeveloped land. Later she attended an academy for young ladies and taught school for one year.

Due to the demanding nature of farm work and the living conditions, Mary Jane and Chloe May established a set of values that permeated the life of their family. Because medical assistance was virtually non-existent, cleanliness was extremely important. Church groups liked to come to their house for meetings because the food was good and the house was clean; there was always a white tablecloth on the dining table. Second, honesty was essential in both personal matters and business. Goods were bought and sold with a handshake and your reputation was paramount in dealing with others. Your word was your bond. Third, Mary Jane and Chloe May took pride in helping those in the community. They had respect for the feelings of others and a concern for those in need. To be productive and a responsible neighbor and citizen you needed to be tough but fair and ready to lend a helping hand both to people and animals when it was required. Obviously,

hard work, discipline, and organization were of paramount importance. There were a great number of daily tasks that had to be done no
matter the weather or how you felt. There was routine established of
getting up early, washing, dressing, and doing the initial chores before
breakfast that Mary Jane, Chloe May, and later Mary Ann, kept up
until they were no longer physically able.

Chloe had a particular friendship with a family and their son who lived
a short distance away. It blossomed to the point that they had talked
of marriage. However, it was not to be. The family wanted the son to
attend medical school, become a doctor and marriage at this time was
not in their plans. At the time, Chloe was devastated. Later in life he
told Chloe that he wished he had married her despite his family ob-
jections. Through family friends she met Robert Coons of Dearborn,
Missouri. Robert was a lawyer and surveyor and at the time lived in
Platte City, Missouri, even though he was born at Camden Point. They
were married in 1900 when she was 22 and he was 27. He joined with
Francis Wilson in a law practice in Platte City.

Robert's family background is interesting. I do not have information
that authenticates the direct linkage between Joseph the German immigrant and Henry the American settler but what is presented is pre-
sumed to be accurate.

My research into Robert's family background provides interesting insight, both into our family's history and early American Family history in general. Though the record is not complete, Robert's genealogy
can be traced to Germany in the early 18th century. In the early 1700's
Governor Spotswood of Virginia discovered deposits of iron ore on several large tracts of land he owned. After spending a good deal of time
getting Queen Anne of England's permission to develop the property
and working out the financial share she would receive, he arranged to
have a group of German miners come to America and bring with them

the requisite technology to convert the ore to usable product. The result was that in 1714 he brought 12 families from the village of Musen in the province of Nassau-Siegen in Westphalia, Germany to Virginia. Musen was a clean little town of about 2,000 with neat homes and intelligent people in one of the thriftiest areas of Germany. It also had one of the most celebrated iron mines in the country. This became the first German colony that came to Virginia. Settling at Germanna in April 1714, the Governor built them cabins and a blockhouse. He also provided the means to mine the ore and build a blast furnace.

The head of one of the families was Joseph Cuntze (Coons). He and the other miners continued to work for the Governor until 1720 when they moved to Germantown (Fanquier County) owing to some dissatisfaction with the Governor's treatment of them. Here they leased large tracts of land and went into farming. Joseph died in Stafford County, VA in 1731. His son Joseph, Jr. continued to farm in Virginia, as did his son Jacob who was recruited into the Continental army in 1781. He fought in the Revolutionary war as a Lieutenant from Culpepper County, VA. His father had deeded him 127 ½ acres of land near the little fork of the Rappahannock River where he lived with his family including son Henry. Henry married Mary Grimsley and started the family migration west, moving to Bourbon County, Kentucky. Their son Joseph F. Coons was born in 1819 in Kentucky, married Katherine Gaines, and relocated to Platte County, Missouri where Robert's father John was born in 1847. John married Caroline Whitten with Robert Newton being born in 1873.

Prior to entering the practice of law, Robert had been nominated to be Surveyor of Platte County, Missouri. He won the popular vote and was re-nominated without opposition. He was very popular and was described as being quiet but with a jovial disposition. On a Surveying trip in 1905, he contracted typhoid fever. As his health continued to weaken, he was taken by his brothers and Chloe May from Platte City to the family farm in Excelsior Springs, Missouri. He died at the farm on December 23, just six months after the birth of his daughter, Mary Angeline, my mother. Just like her mother Mary Jane, Chloe was a widow at age 27 with two small children.

Robert was a member of the family for just five years, but he left a lasting legacy. Obviously he and Chloe's children, Robert Sidney and Mary Angeline, were a large part of his legacy. Throughout his short life his focus was on education, both formal and informal. He was a student of the law and at the time of his death had a large collection of books relating to the law. He was also a student of history, science, and literature among others. In addition to his law books, his collection included the complete works of Shakespeare, Thomas Babington Macaulay's five-volume *The History of* England, Edward Gibbon's six-volume *The History of the Decline and Fall of the Roman Empire,* and 49 volumes of *The Harvard Classics,* all of which are now in my home.

It is interesting to speculate at this point as to whether Robert's interest in books and knowledge was purely entertainment and a way to describe or see the world in the way it is or was or rather to suppose that books were a means to stimulate the imagination to visualize what the world could become. He lived in an interesting time of transformation. Attitudes were changing in America from the class- system of Europe with values and wealth dependent on your family lineage to one of honesty, work ethic, innovation and confidence in the future. Books are a way to stimulate the imagination to think outside the box, if you will, and to be a part of creating the future rather than living in the past and leaving a legacy of old values and outdated thinking. We will never know but I think his books are in a way a challenge to us to think ahead and be an active part of the future.

With really no other place to go, Chloe May, and her children, Robert Sidney and Mary Angeline, went back to the farm to live with her mother and brothers – Bill, Joe and Ralph. It could have been a difficult transition for all involved but Mary Jane at once decided that she would manage the farm operations and Chloe would manage the house. With Chloe following in and building upon the previously mentioned values set in place by Mary Jane, along with Mary Jane's business acumen, the family became successful under these two strong women. An important aspect of the enduring family legacy is the emphasis on the holiday season that was codified during this time. Anticipation was always high coming into the Thanksgiving and Christmas seasons. There was a large rock fireplace that had a Yule log and it was used repeatedly to cook meat and vegetables. To prepare for the big days, a particular chicken would be fed and fattened so that it would be plump and juicy providing not only for the meat but broth for the dressing and gravy as well. There would be pumpkin and mince pie and always Grandmother's famous biscuits cooked in the wood stove. Sweets made specifically for the holidays included sugar candy, horehound, and fudge. Syrup was made from their maple tree sap.

For Christmas woolen stocking were hung by the fireplace and stuffed with candy, fruit and nuts. The Christmas tree was cut from their forest and decorated with strings of popcorn or braided material. Gifts were handmade, such a mittens and socks made of wool from their own sheep. Mary Angeline would receive a stuffed doll sewn of cloth. Robert Sidney would receive a knife or hand carved slingshot. In the evening, Ralph would play his violin and they would sing their favorite carols. Though they did not enjoy great material wealth, the family never lacked for what they needed. They were genuinely close to one another especially during the holidays. Thanksgiving and Christmas became a significant time for family, faith, and fun – traditions and values that are still important to this day.

The farm was a busy place in those early days of Mary Angeline's life. There was not strict discipline per se, but there were definitive rules and practices that she was expected to follow. One was that she was to stay out of the way of the workers and not go to the barn unless accompanied by one of the family members. She amused herself by playing with her stuffed dolls, several kittens that Uncle Joe brought her, a pet pigeon, or a make-believe dollhouse she constructed out of rocks. Mary Angeline's most treasured moments occurred when Mary Jane would read stories to her from a set of children's books.

Mary Angeline's first school was a two-room house located through the pasture and across the creek. Children of all ages were taught in those two rooms with discipline being severe at times. She remembers Robert Sidney getting a whipping for something he did not deserve or even know about.

During this period Uncle Bill finished high school and then went to the University of Missouri. While Bill was a Student at Mizzo, there was a popular song with the name Mary Ann in it. When he can home he began calling his niece Mary Ann; it stuck and from then on she has always used and been known as Mary Ann. Bill was a star on the University football team as a running back. He was featured in articles that appeared in the New York Times, Chicago Tribune, and St. Louis Post Gazette. The experience also left him with two injured knees that gave him trouble the rest of his life. He graduated with a degree in Animal Husbandry and returned to the farm with the intent of expanding the dairy operation.

In this pursuit Bill acquired additional milk cows and started the process of building the large stone barn that still stands on the property. The stone came from a quarry near the farm and the tongue and groove oak ceiling from trees on the property. The ceiling was made in this way so straw or hay from the upper floor would not fall into the milk. Shortly after the work started Bill got an offer to go into partnership and manage a cattle ranch in Hoehne, Colorado and Raton,

New Mexico. He accepted leaving completion of the barn to Ralph and Mary Jane.

In Hoehne Bill married Margret Lloyd and in 1915, their daughter Mary Jo, was born. Unfortunately when Mary Jo was seven months old, her mother was killed in a car/train accident, and she was badly injured. The car that Mary Jo was riding in stalled on the train track with a train coming. In order to save Mary Jo, her mother threw her out of the window. On learning of this tragedy, Chloe May along with Mary Ann and Robert Sidney, took the train to Hoehne to assume the responsibility of making a home for Bill and carrying for Mary Jo. In 1916 they moved to the property in Raton; six years later Bill passed away on Easter Sunday from pneumonia. Chloe then closed the cattle and diary business and moved with her family back to the farm near Excelsior Springs, Missouri.

In the meantime, Joe was pursuing a medical career. He was the quintessential country doctor. Although he did not have a degree, he treated all varieties of animals, and he was always on call if someone had an ailment or injury that he could handle. World War I broke out in Europe in 1914 and in 1917 President Wilson signed into law the conscription act. Rather than be drafted, Joe enlisted in the Medical Corp of the Army, and was one of the first of the United States troops to be sent to France. It was unfortunate timing as Joe had just been accepted to understudy a Doctor in his quest for more formal medical training. During the War, Joe was living in the trenches and treating many wounded. When armistice was declared, he worked in Belgium and Northern France resettling refugees and treating their various medical conditions. He returned in 1919 but was suffering from what we now call Post Traumatic Stress Disorder.

Later, in World War II, Mary Jo's husband was in the First Marine Division participating in all the Pacific Island invasions. He was one of only two survivors of his company to return alive. He, too, suffered from PTSD to the point where the authorities said that they could no longer protect Mary Jo or her two children and advised her to leave. She did and returned to the farm from their home at that time in California. Joe, her Uncle, did not function well either on trying to reenter productive society after World War I. He went to Colorado had a number of jobs and eventually died in 1933.

Mary Ann was 10 years of age when they went to Colorado and New Mexico. There were several immediate adjustments. Fruit and fresh vegetables were scarce or non-existent, replaced by beans, peppers and tortillas. School was also quite an adjustment. She and Robert Sidney were the only white protestant children in the classroom and they struggled to make friends. They were alone in a strange place. On her birthday, June 9th, the wind was blowing, dust was everywhere, and she was more than a little sad. It was then that a package arrived from her Grandmother, Mary Jane, which contained a beautiful gold ring with an agate setting. The sun shone and a big smile came over her face. The ring never left her finger until she gifted the ring to her great granddaughter, Carly, some 90 years later. To make some money and to build muscles to later play football, Robert Sidney worked on the railroad running between Raton and Hoehne. Eventually the family became acclimated to their surroundings and enjoyed many new and exciting experiences. Mary Ann likes to tell of the cattle drives to market with the Mexican cowboys riding with Bill, and the encounters they shared.

As Joe enlisted in 1917, so did Robert Sidney. He was 15 at the time, but told the recruiters he was 18. So one day he simply did not come home from school; he was shipped off to Texas and enrolled in flight school. Chloe May was furious. She tried to get the enlistment annulled but to no avail. Over the next two years he tried to ferry three planes to the East Coast for transfer to France, but for various reasons the planes crashed each time. Fortunately he was not seriously injured. After the war he pursued a business education and received a CPA. He worked for a public accounting firm, Arthur Young, and then participated in the formation of Interstate Bakeries, retiring as Vice President and Treasurer.

When Mary Ann and Chloe May returned to the farm in 1922, Mary Ann completed her senior year in Excelsior Springs high school and was then off to Hardin College in Mexico, Missouri. She received a two-year associate degree and returned to the farm. By this time the house had an indoor ice refrigerator and an 8-party line telephone. Technological innovation was slowly making its way to the country but the farm still had oil lamps, well water and wood stoves to heat and to cook.

A year later in 1923 Chloe May was offered the opportunity to work at the Clay County State Bank in Excelsior Springs as a bookkeeper. She accepted, but continued to live at the farm and to help her mother with the farm work. That was the beginning of a 31-year career at the bank where she retired as a teller at the age of 78. One of her customers was a semi-precious gem dealer, who in appreciation for her friendship and service over the years, gave her a large aquamarine stone before she retired, which I later had made into a necklace.

On July 30, 1926, Robert Sidney married Ella Berenice Sloan in Excelsior Springs. Berenice's ancestors can be traced back to Christian Wyman and his wife Ann Maria who migrated from lower Pennsylvania in the late 1770's into Indiana Territory and then into Missouri in the early 1800's by way of the Ohio and Missouri Rivers. Christian brought with him what was considered at that time a considerable amount of money, some of which he used to buy land. He built his home there and also gave the land to build the Baptist church, which was given the name Pisgah. The first preacher was "Uncle Bobby" James, the father of

Jesse and Frank James. The James brothers were famous Confederate guerrillas turned bank and train robbers in the 1870's and 1880's.

Christian's son Anthony was one of the co-founders of the city of Excelsior Springs. A daughter, Julie, was born to Bob and Berenice on June 22, 1941. She married William Buckingham, an orthopedic surgeon, on July 25, 1964. Bill was the son of Ruth Busch, RN, and William Buckingham, Sr. MD. He was a well-known Kansas City thoracic surgeon who pioneered advances in TB surgery. The Buckingham fountain in Chicago is named after Clarence Buckingham, one of Bill's relatives, who was a businessman, avid art collector and philanthropist. The fountain is made of pink marble and four pairs of sea horses surround it. Each pair of sea horses represents a state bordering Lake Michigan. They shoot a jet stream of water 150 feet into the air, effectively turning the fountain into a liquid skyscraper. His sister, Kate Buckingham, gave it to the city of Chicago in 1927 in honor of Clarence. Both Julie and Bill graduated from the University of Missouri, were long time residents of Jacksonville, FL and now live in Santa Fe, NM. They had two sons, William III, born July 15, 1966, and Brendhan, born October 21, 1968. William graduated from Florida State University and New York University Film School. He is a successful action film producer living in Los Angeles, California. Recently he and his company created the award winning Budweiser commercial featuring the Clydesdale horses for the 2013 Super Bowl and the round-the-world commercials for Chevrolet featured in the 2014 Olympics. Brendhan graduated from Tulane and Oregon Universities. He specializes in emergency room medicine practicing in Birmingham, Alabama.

The house and farm that Mary Jane built became a sanctuary in every sense of the word. It was a meeting place for business, church, and family. The house and farm were especially important to the family during the holidays as a space to pass on traditions. It would also provide safe haven and comfort during difficult times, such as when Robert Newton passed away.

Robert N. Coons, 1904

Robert Sidney & Mary Ann Coons

Mary Jane Carothers & Chloe May Coons, 1950

Ralph Carothers, 1936

Chloe May Coons 100th Birthday in 1978
Julie (Coons) Buckingham, Mary Ann Frieling, Gerald Frieling, Chloe
May Coons, Robert Sidney Coons, Jerry Frieling, Berenice Coons

Mary Ann (Coons) Frieling 100th Birthday - 2005

CHAPTER 4

Marriage – Frieling & Coons

There was only one place significant enough to host such an important union for the family. As the sun was setting on July 31, 1928, Mary Ann and Jerry were married under the big oak tree in the front yard of the farmhouse. It had been raining for several days before the ceremony. The road to the farm was so muddy that guests had to leave their cars and walk to the wedding. Wedding guests would frequently recount Tom Seburn, Jerry's good friend from the University of Michigan, leaving his car and walking through the mud carrying a large floor lamp as a wedding present. At the time of their marriage, Mary Ann had never lived in a house that had electricity, running water, indoor plumbing, mechanical refrigeration or central heating. As described earlier, the living conditions at the farm were still fairly primitive. Each bedroom had a chamber pot and the beds were warmed in the cold winters using coals from the wood stoves.

After the ceremony Jerry and Mary Ann drove to Chicago and stayed at the Palmer House Hotel. They then went to Grand Rapids to meet the rest of the Frieling side of the family, along with additional friends. It made for a beautiful and meaningful honeymoon. On the way back they stopped at the farm to pick up Mary Ann's belongings and then traveled to Northeast Kansas City, Missouri, where they would make their first home.

They chose that location because it was close to the Division of the Kansas City Public Service Company where Jerry worked. Two years later on April 29, 1930 I was born. Although I was technically a "depression baby" through the family's planning, hard work, and a little good fortune, we were better off than most. My father had a secure job providing transportation services to the public and we were not that far away from fresh fruit, vegetables, milk and meat from the farm.

It is through our family situation that we viewed the economic and political events of the time period. In 1932 Franklin D. Roosevelt was elected President of the country for the first time. There were 11 million people jobless in the United States, which provided the motivation for broad sweeping legislation. The WPA, a job/works program, was started, in addition to Social Security, which provided for income after retirement. Being connected to both the urban Kansas City and the rural farm, we were able to see the benefits and the consequences of FDR's programs. This was especially true of his farm policies, which even divided the farming community. I can remember stories of the family sitting around the kitchen table at the farm debating the President's farm policy. Grandmother Chloe was a strong advocate of the free market system and was opposed philosophically to government intervention or subsidies. She also saw first-hand the consequences of the more controversial policies, such as Secretary of Agriculture Henry A Wallace's support of slaughtering and discarding pigs. For years afterwards each time I called her, the first words were "what do you think of the farm policy".

I remember certain events in those early years, both good and bad, that left a lasting impression. One such memory was attending the World's Fair in Chicago in 1933. It was a thrilling event when I got a Texaco fire chief hat. I also remember a stray dog – Trixie. I held a pancake behind my back to attract her from the other kids in the neighborhood. Trixie and I become best pals for the next 14 years. Sometime after my fifth birthday I came down with scarlet fever, which resulted in the house being quarantined, and most of my skin pealing off from the high fever. Also, in 1933 Hitler was named German Chancellor, and after 14 years prohibition ended. Poland was invaded by Germany in 1939 and thus began World War II.

When I reached six years of age in 1936, an event took place that certainly changed the course of my life and provides strong evidence just how important education has been and continues to be to our family. At a very early age, my Grandmother Coons continually impressed on my Mother and me the importance of a good education and in particular, a college degree. Northeast Kansas City was a working class section of the city where very few young people went to college or became professionals. In light of this, Mother researched where the best educational and social-economic areas were located in the city and was determined to move there.

When it was time for me to enroll in the first grade we moved to the Southwest section of the city and into the Border Star Elementary and Southwest High School districts. At that time virtually 100% of the students graduated high school and went onto a four-year college or university with many in Ivy League or Big Ten schools. The transition could have been a difficult one, but the principal was instrumental in facilitating this process. I also used my athletic ability as a means to integrate into the social life of the school, which turned out to be very important. The friends I made and the education I received established my future direction. I will never forget it or the debt of gratitude I owe my Mother for taking the initiative.

Mary Ann (Coons) Frieling wedding picture, 1928

CHAPTER 5

Adolescence - 1930's & 40's

Mother believed strongly in helping people in the community and this manifested itself in many ways. In the 1930's the Country was in the midst of the great depression. I can remember the dust storms and having to walk to school with a wet cloth mask over my face. I also remember the bread lines and Mother giving food to people that came to the house hungry. One of the best examples of our family's involvement in the community, up to that time, was scouting.

Scouting was important to our family because it stood for similar values. It is the stated goal of Scouting "to contribute to the development of young people in achieving their full physical, intellectual, social and spiritual potentials as individuals, as responsible citizens and as members of their local, national and international communities." The emphasis on the outdoors, on survival skills, and on respect for the land and its connections with Native Americans, resonated with our family values. Mother became a den mother for the Cub Scout troop, which consisted of most of my friends from school. Later, I joined the Boy Scouts at the local Congregational Church. One of my friends in Cub Scouting lost his mother by suicide. My mother took him under her wing and was a great support for him during those difficult times. He later became a respected international architect and he never forgot the kindness that mother showed him. During most summers I attended Scout Camp, which I thoroughly enjoyed especially learning camping and nature skills.

I became an Eagle Scout and received a medal from the national organization in recognition, in their words, "of performing a life saving act protecting several younger children at a busy intersection".

In addition to going to scout camp, I always spent time in Michigan during the summer. We went to Grand Rapids and Grand Haven, Michigan. Those were enjoyable times swimming in Lake Michigan, visiting the Coast Guard station, and hanging out with the Grandparents. Another memorable event was taking the train alone from Kansas City to Detroit, Michigan in 1940, when I was 10, to visit my Aunts and Uncles. When I was boarding the train my father gave me an extra dollar. At the end of the trip the porter asked me if my Dad had given me anything for him. I said yes and handed him a nickel.

This was the era of the big bands, which meant we all attended dancing school with the goal of becoming accomplished in ballroom dancing. I still remember the white gloves. This was also the time that mother thought I should learn to play a musical instrument, so I took trumpet lessons at the conservatory of music in Kansas City and joined the school band. I enjoyed the experience but I got into a fight on the basketball court in high school and loosened my front teeth. That was the end of my musical career.

I was washing the family car on Sunday December 7, 1941 when Pearl Harbor was bombed and ushered the United States into the war. My fourth & fifth grade teachers enlisted in the Women's Army Corps shortly afterwards. They were two of the best teachers I ever had, including my college professors. I never heard from them again.

The allies invaded France on June 6, 1944 (D-Day), which signaled the beginning of the end of World War II. President Roosevelt died in 1945 with Harry Truman taking over and authorized the dropping of the first atomic bomb on Hiroshima, Japan. The Japanese surrendered shortly afterwards.

Our class went straight into high school from the seventh grade, skipping the eighth. It was not a good idea considering our level of maturity, both physically and emotionally, but on the other hand, I would not have met my future wife. Our high school was the best in the city. It was managed more like a college. We had fraternities and sororities, some open classrooms and a wide range of course options. Athletics were outstanding. I lettered in the three major sports; football, basketball and track. Our senior year, we were city champions in football and track. This was a big deal where we got to wear our letters on white sweaters. The fraternity I joined, Delta Sigma, was composed of mostly of my friends from grade school and the athletic teams from high school. They were a great bunch of guys and many of the friendships have lasted until the present time. Like college, the social life was centered around the fraternities and sororities. We had dances most Friday nights with the usual spring and winter formals as a part of the mix.

One of my favorite teachers in high school was Ms. Guyer. She was the history teacher and instilled in me a lifelong interest in history. To this day I prefer to read a good non-fiction book with a historical content rather than a serial fiction novel. At the time she thought I should concentrate more on academics, particularly history, rather than athletics and social pursuits. She was probably right, but I always told her you have to have balance in your life. Our family has always stressed the importance of a well-rounded education – academics, but also athletics, travel, and socialization.

In 1940, I was invited to a family's home for dinner; mother, father, and daughter. They had an out of town guest staying with them who happened to be Walt Disney. He graciously sketched Mickey Mouse on a white cocktail napkin and I treasured that for a long period of time. I don't know where it is. He talked about his desire to make Mickey Mouse and associated characters interesting and liked by children and adults alike.

An important part of my educational experiences was the jobs that I had in the summers of my high school and college years. These were varied and certainly gave me insight into various companies and industries. For example, I ran grain samples to the floor of the Board of Trade grain exchange, was a construction worker on the six story Sears building, and a tool & die apprentice with Westinghouse Electric manufacturing their first jet engine – the J-34 for the Navy. For any young person I believe that internships are a key component of their experience and should be acquired at every opportunity.

I also worked in an auto repair shop when I memorably acquired my first car. It was a 1931 Chevrolet Coupe with a rumble seat. In the color of the era, it was black with a red leather rumble seat and on-the-floor stick shift. I loved that car, but it had mechanical brakes instead of hydraulic, which on occasion would freeze. It was very frustrating when this happened. I learned to drive at the farm in Ralph's model "A" Ford. It was quite a thrill negotiating rocks and ruts in the field with a stick shift. I've never forgotten the lessons. It was probably my experiences working in the auto repair shop and at Westinghouse that led me to become a mechanical engineer.

As often as possible we joined with Mary Jane, Chloe May and Ralph at Thanksgiving celebrating the holiday at either our home or with Bob, Berenice and Julie in their home. Mary Jane died in 1952, so afterwards it was just Chloe May and Ralph. It was a time to reconnect and enjoy some of the family stories and traditions. Two of the family stories involve me during a couple of my many trips to the farm. After they closed the dairy business they turned the separator house, which was used to separate the cream from the milk, into a grain storage shed. One day when I went in there, a mouse ran up my leg inside my pants, not once, but twice. The family jokes that I broke the high jump record that day. On another day, I went into the smoke house in back of the main house where they smoked all kinds of meat and fowl for preservation, only to have a large black snake drop from on top of the door to around my neck. I think I broke the 100-yard dash record on that occasion.

The war was over in 1945 but the draft was still in effect with no college deferments. One of my good friends, Charlie Ferguson, and I decided that we did not want to be drafted so we joined the Navy's flight program at the Olathe Naval Air Station. It actually turned out to be a good decision as we only went to drills once a month. In 1950 when they instituted college deferments, we dropped the program, as by that time, we were both in college.

Also in 1950 North Korea invaded the South, which started the Korean War. In 1948 the State of Israel came into existence, which resulted in great controversy within the Middle Eastern Arab states. That situation has yet to be fully resolved.

For college, I only applied to two schools: University of Michigan, where my father went, and University of Kansas, where most of my friends were going. The friends won out and over the summer of 1947, there was a number of fraternity rush parties, which further sealed the deal for Kansas. On entering school in the fall, I pledged Sigma Alpha Epsilon (SAE). Our house was at the West end of the campus. Two houses away was the Chi Omega sorority. The SAE pledge class and the Chi O's had a tradition of walking out in the middle of some night, doing minor trashing of the houses and then having a barn dance primarily as a way of meeting people. On this dark night I drove to the Chi O house in my '31 Chevy, saw a girl standing outside, and invited her to go with me. That girl turned out to be my future wife, Joan Lee Bigham.

I graduated from Kansas in 1951 with a Bachelors degree in Mechanical Engineering. I was named the Outstanding ME graduate for that year and also received recognition for winning the University's technical paper and speech contest. I took second place with that technical paper in the Midwest University regional contest losing out because the judges were not aware that it was an original development. One of the judges came up to me afterwards and said if I had planted someone in the audience to ask the question I would have won. Live and learn! In 1986 I received the Distinguished Engineering Service Award from the School of Engineering and in 2011, I was named their person of the year and addressed the graduating seniors. My successes are my family's successes. Their origins can be traced back to my parents moving into a better school district, to my mother being my Den mother, experiences at the farm, to holidays with the family, to Joan at the "Chi O" house and all the sacrifices made and values instilled in me by my family and loved ones.

Jerry Frieling in football letter sweater with Trixie, 1946

Jerry Frieling & Joan Bigham with 1931 Chevrolet, 1947

CHAPTER 6

Early years – The Bigham & Linville Families

The history of the Bigham and Linville families and that of Joan's mother's, the Brown, Burgess and Dail families comes courtesy of Jay Kimmel, Joan's cousin, who has done an inordinate amount of genealogy research. Although family legend has their origin in England, we start their story with Nathaniel Bigham and his wife Rebecca White in Winchester, Franklin County Tennessee, where he purchased property in 1811. Nathaniel died in 1818. Rebecca was born in Virginia on October 17, 1773, moving sometime later to Franklin County, Tennessee, where she married Nathaniel. They had a number of children, including John Bigham. After Nathaniel's death, Rebecca and her family moved to Lawrence County, Alabama. Sometime between 1830 and 1834, they moved to Platte County, Missouri - the same county where my Grandfather, Robert and Grandmother, Chloe May Coons lived after they were married. Rebecca died March 8, 1852 in Platte County where she lived with her son John. She is buried at the Old Campground Cemetery.

John, who was born on April 4, 1808, married Lessarah (Sarah) Evans on February 14, 1833, in Johnson County, Missouri. He later moved to the New Market area of Platte County where he acquired land at the time of the formation of the county from Indian Territory. He became an elder of the Cumberland Presbyterian Church. Based on family stories, John was a wealthy slave owner who moved to Texas during the Civil War. He died at home in DeKalb, Buchannan County, Missouri on October 15, 1888 and is also buried in the Old Campground cemetery.

49

John and Sarah had 10 children, one of whom was Samuel Franklin Bigham, known as Frank. He was born in 1835. On March 13, 1866, he married Nancy Ann Linville, who was born in 1848.

The Linville's were from Sussex, England, and were probably Quakers. They came to America on the first voyage of William Penn, arriving in Pennsylvania in 1682. There were 22 ships on that voyage, taking about 5 months to cross the Atlantic. Members of the family then took "The Great Wagon Road" to North Carolina on to Tennessee and then "The Applegate Trail" to Missouri. Nancy's father was Abraham Linville, born January 8, 1805, in Tennessee, and married Nancy Trapp, who was born in Tennessee in 1808. Abraham took the family to Missouri where Nancy was born. Nancy and Frank's first child, Atta, was the first child born to white parents in the area of Wyandotte County, Kansas previously occupied by the Delaware Indians. On July 4, 1866, the Delaware Indians signed a new treaty in which they agreed to sell their remaining tribal lands to the Missouri River Railroad Company (Missouri Pacific) for $2.50 an acre, and move to the Cherokee Nation in Indian Territory. That move was made in the winter of 1867 and the spring of 1868 with much hardship and numerous deaths. In light of this situation, 175 Delaware Indians chose to give up their tribal relations, become United States citizens, and retain their 80-acre allotments in Wyandotte and Leavenworth Counties.

Milton Jackson (Jack or MJ) Bigham was born to Frank and Nancy on January 20, 1867, near Weston, Platte County, Missouri. He moved with his parents before he was three years old to Wyandotte County, Kansas, where he lived the rest of his life. He was a farmer and dairyman. On September 24, 1890, he married Emma Marie Rothert (born February 10, 1871). They started their married life on the 50-acre Rothert farm. Subsequently, he bought what was known as the "English" property, which increased his total acreage to 149. MJ, along with his parents and two of his sisters, were charter members of the Bethel United Presbyterian Church when it was organized in 1895.

Frank Allen, Joan's father, was born to Emma and Jack on January 29, 1898. When he reached adulthood, Frank and his father went into the dairy business together. Jack owned the herd and produced the milk. Frank managed the retail operations selling most of the milk in Kansas City, Kansas. Later he bought the homestead from Jack and continued in the dairy business. He married Susan Emmaline (Susie) Brown on June 19, 1927. Susie was born on April 16, 1904 to Robert E. Lee Brown and Zena Ella Dail.

Frank was very successful in his dairy, real estate, and various business ventures, but he always espoused the importance of family and community over the blind pursuit of money. He continuously advised his children, family, and everyone who would listen to look at the familial relationships and values of potential friends and/or spouses. His favorite expression was "If you want to improve the quality of your herd, get a bull with good bloodlines".

He used his knowledge and expertise as a developer to further his business as well as the community. Frank owned and managed several rental properties. He developed the Indian Wood sub-division on what was formerly the Wise property, across the road from the original Bigham homestead. He supported building programs at the church and school. He invested in War Bonds on behalf of his children's selling initiatives along with many philanthropic projects. Frank left a lasting legacy by selling his property, before he died, to the Catholic Hospital Corporation. The hospital was constructed for the community on pastureland adjacent to the family home and turned the farmhouse into the nurses' quarters. The hospital has expanded since then and is still in operation today. At the time of his death on November 28, 1980, Frank was a director of the Wyandotte Bank, on the board of the Wyandotte County Farm Bureau, and a member of Rotary and the Bethel United Presbyterian Church.

Frank Allen & Susie Bigham

CHAPTER 7

Early years – The Brown, Dail & Burgess Families

Joan's mother, Susie Bigham, was the daughter of Zena Dail. Zena was the daughter of Charles Calhoun(C.C.) Dail, born January 11, 1851, and Nancy Ann Burgess, born March 5, 1855. C.C.'s mother was the sister to the mother of President Zachary Taylor. C.C. lived in Kentucky, Ohio, Missouri and Kansas and was a soldier in the Ohio Calvary serving under Colonel George Custer from 1870 to 1872. C.C. and Nancy were married on August 22, 1875 in New Market, Missouri. When he was 11, both of C.C.'s parents died. He was put in a foster home while his two brothers went to fight in the Civil War. C.C. struggled with the horrible conditions and eventually ran away.

During his time on his own, he wandered into the lobby of a hotel in Kentucky. He met a man who said he looked just like his father, who was a circuit court judge and asked if he would like to meet him. He said he would but thought the man was actually his brother so left and headed toward his sister's house. On the way he came to a fork in the road. Stopping to take a nap he had a dream that told him which road to take and that he would come to a house with his sister laying in a coffin inside the house. When he awoke he did what his dream told him and it turned out to be true. Through the years C.C. became a successful self-taught lawyer and poet. Once he wrote an entire case in poetry and filed it in the Wyandotte County Courthouse. The case involved a man with a dispute against a railroad. It was settled out of court.

Nancy Burgess was the daughter of Reuben Burgess, born in 1814 in Lawrence County, Kentucky and Mary Donohue, born in 1823. They lived in Kentucky, Missouri and Kansas. They lived a life of wealth and privilege; they had 10 children and 196 slaves. Reuben was the child of William Burgess, born in 1775, and Sarah Ann Strother, born in 1783. William's father was Edward Burgess, born 1744 in Montgomery County, Virginia, who along with ten other young men from the area, including Davy Crockett, acted as spies against the Native Americans during the French and Indian War, warning the citizens when there was an uprising to go to the safety of the forts.

Edward served in the Continental Army during the Revolution from 1776 to 1781. He was a scout with Daniel Boone and later, as a soldier and militiaman with Colonel Buford of the Virginia Regiment. They fought in prominent battles such as Clap's Mill, Ramsour's Mill and Camden (known as Gates Defeat). He was honorably discharged in Hillsborough, North Carolina, and again joined with Daniel Boone in Kentucky, scouting the western territory. Because of Edward's and other family member's service in the Continental Army, this service became the basis of the application of Susie and her daughter, Joyce, into the Daughters of the American Revolution.

Susie's father was Robert E. Lee Brown, born October 11, 1865. He was obviously named after General Robert E. Lee, who surrendered the Confederate Army of Northern Virginia to General U.S. Grant at Appomattox Courthouse on April 9, 1865. Mr. Brown's father was Washington Henry Brown and his mother was Susan E. Pierce, who was born in 1829 and died in 1904. Susan was the second cousin of Franklin Pierce, the 14th President of the United States.

Franklin Pierce was born in Hillsboro, New Hampshire in 1804 and died October 8, 1869. At 48, he became the youngest president up to that time and impressed all who met him because of his good looks and brilliant speaking ability. Pierce took part in the Mexican – American War and became a brigadier general in the Army. His private law practice in his home state was so successful that he was offered several important positions, which he turned down. He gained the support of the Democratic Party because of his support of the Compromise of 1850, which sought to find a solution to the slavery dispute, and of his fine record in both the House and Senate representing New Hampshire. Despite a reputation as an able politician and a likable man, during Pierce's presidency (1853-1857), he served only as a moderator among the increasingly bitter factions that were driving the nation towards civil war.

Washington Henry Brown was a prosperous farmer who was born in 1831 and died in 1905. He was also a successful breeder of racehorses. Near the end of his life he completed a magnificent home on land that the government had bought from the Indians. It was a two and one-half story Georgian Revival house that was said to be the finest in western Wyandotte County in the tradition of the "gentleman farmer." The house was passed on to his son, R.E.L. Brown, on his death. He and his wife Zena lived in the house until the late 1940's. Frank and Susie were married there in 1927 and their children spent many pleasant days staying at the house during summer vacations. It was featured in a 1988 book on Kansas City architecture.

It was an important and lasting example of the family's early emphasis on education when Susie graduated from the University of Kansas in 1925. She then taught school for a year before marrying Frank Allen. They had five children, four of which survived: Joan Lee born July 30, 1929, Joyce Marie born July 19, 1930, Frank Allen Jr. born November 25, 1931 and Nancy Sue born September 22, 1937. Nancy was married and died in 1965. Joyce married Harold Ogden and together they had four children; Jane, Dane and Brad who live in the Kansas City – Lawrence, Kansas area and John who lives in Castle Rock, Colorado. Joyce died of cancer in 1996. Frank Jr. married Harriet McGaugh on December 20, 1956. They have two children, Frank Allen III and Sydney. Frank Jr. was a member of the Oklahoma State basketball team under coach Hank Iba. He became a teacher and college level basketball and golf coach. He is now retired and living with Harriet in Kansas City, Missouri; and will soon move to Scottsdale, Arizona. Harriet was also a teacher and an accomplished artist. She too is retired but continues an active painting career. Harriet was born in Oklahoma and both she and Frank graduated from Oklahoma State University, as did their daughter Sydney, who was on the OSU varsity golf team. Frank III graduated from the University of Missouri (Kansas City) in 1980 with a degree in Physical Education and a minor in Math. He taught middle and high school students for a number of years.

A special memory for John, Bob and Nancy was when they would go to the Bigham house over an Easter weekend. They, together with all the cousins, would color Easter eggs deciding who did the best job. On Easter Sunday, after church, they would go back to the farmhouse where someone would have hidden the eggs. A big egg hunt would follow complete with other presents and lots of laughter at dinner as to who found the most eggs. It was a good occasion for the families to get together especially since the cousins lived in Indian Woods, Papa Frank's development across the road from the farm.

Robert E. Lee & Zena Brown

Advertisement for Bigham Dairy
Joan & Joyce Bigham – 1932

CHAPTER 8

Adolescence - Joan

Joan remembers that growing up the Bigham household was happy and full of activities. The family always began with the entire family sitting down for breakfast together after Mr. Bigham completed his milk route. The children had Shetland ponies that they shared with their friends. Joan's pony was Mitzie, which she rode on several occasions in the opening ceremony of the American Royal horse show carrying the flag. The family had an ice skating pond, which was also a popular center for family and friends. Susie could watch all the fun from the large window in the farmhouse. Susie had live-in help during those years, which usually meant an additional person to play hockey or another body to push down the sledding hill.

Joan really blossomed in high school through National Honor Society, editor of the yearbook, Homecoming Queen, various sports, and other activities. She became president of every organization in which she was a member. That people-centered and administrative ability carried on into college where she was President of her sorority, Chi Omega, and the Inter-Fraternity council. She attended the University of Kansas graduating in Liberal Arts in 1951. In 1950 between her junior and senior years, she had an opportunity to attend the National Convention of Chi Omega at the Greenbrier Resort in White Sulfur Springs, West Virginia. Keeping the independent family spirit alive, she went alone on the train from Kansas City to Virginia.

Like her mother, after graduating from KU she taught school for a year before she was married. We were engaged in December 1951, after which I wrote her parents a letter setting forth my goals for the future and my ability to take care of their daughter. I had two goals; one was to become a member of the Young Presidents Organization and the second was to be the CEO (Chief Executive Officer) of a New York Stock Exchange listed public company. Joan's mother passed around the letter to all her friends and relatives. I'm sure it was a source of amusement at times, but the goals set forth in the letter shaped our lives for years to come. Later when I was teaching at the University of Notre Dame, I would have students ask me for advice. I always responded by saying you have to have meaningful goals in your life that you strive to achieve. Goals drive decisions. They certainly did in our life.

Joan Bigham at University of Kansas Graduation, 1951

Jerry Frieling & Joan Bigham at the SAE Winter Formal, 1948

CHAPTER 9
Marriage – Frieling & Bigham

On June 14, 1952, Joan and I were married. The ceremony was held in the First Presbyterian Church in Kansas City, Kansas. Because of Mrs. Bigham's dislike of alcohol we had the reception in the basement of the church. We had the traditional wedding cake with the ladies of the church serving punch. It was really very nice. Joan's Uncle, Wash Brown, slipped me a $100 bill during the reception which, as it turned out blowing four tires to and from Colorado Springs, really came in handy. After a wonderful honeymoon at the Broadmoor in Colorado Springs we went to Beaver, Pennsylvania, where I was with Westinghouse Electric on their Graduate Student Program.

While I worked at the Standard Control Division, Joan ran a nursery school in our home, which was a rented two story duplex. She also sold greeting cards from the Friendly Card Company which helped pay for our first furniture. A few years later, I had forgotten Joan's birthday. I saw her walking toward the house after having a celebratory glass of wine with her friends and quickly realized I was in trouble. I grabbed one of the leftover Friendly cards, gave it to her said "Happy Birthday, let's go out for dinner." Unfortunately, the card said, "Happy Birthday Friend." We didn't make dinner that night but we have had a good laugh about the incident for years.

Overall, I had a great experience while working in Beaver. Westinghouse was introducing a new product and I was selected to make explanatory presentations at several large cities around the country. It was great experience in speaking before large audiences and thinking on your feet. I was having the time of my life, until President Truman put me in 1A draft status. I again joined the Navy, but this time I headed to officer candidate school in Newport, Rhode Island. I had wanted to go to flight training, but my color-blindness kept me from becoming a pilot. Instead, after graduation, we were fortuitously assigned to Civil Engineering Corps officers' school in Port Hueneme, California, and then on to permanent assignment at the Naval Air Station in Corpus Christi, Texas.

I was on active duty in the Navy from mid 1953 to mid 1956. My assignment was with the Public Works Department where we administered large construction contracts like building radar installations and satellite air fields, operating the base infrastructure such as the power and sewer plants and commanding both military and civilian personnel. This was wonderful practical experience for an industrial career later in life. Following in my father's footsteps, I even designed and supervised the base transportation system. To earn a little extra money, I taught in the graduate school at Del Mar College in Corpus Christi, teaching air conditioning design to graduate engineers. It was a three-hour class in the evening. Studying to keep one chapter ahead of the students, I think I learned much more than they did.

In 1954, the first atomic submarine, Nautilus, was launched. I worked on the electrical control system for the Nautilus, which was the reason for my draft deferments prior to being put into IA status.

On January 1, 1955, John Bradley, our first child, was born. Joan went into labor on New Year's Eve and John was subsequently born in the early morning New Year's Day. Both sets of grandparents were very pleased. He was a happy baby with good sleeping and eating habits. As a symbol of the risks we would both take later in life, I introduced John to the Officer's club swimming pool when he was just six months old. We had a great time even though some of the mothers did not think jumping off the diving board was such a good idea.

In mid 1956, my dad resigned from the Kansas City Public Service Company as Vice President of Transportation after 30 years of service. He began a second chapter in his career as a consultant. His years with the Public Service Company brought him in contact with many officials of major companies in the United States and Canada. By government appointment, he served on the National Transportation Board during World War II, and was appointed by the governor to the Missouri State Board of Mediation, which had the power to take over any public service in the event of a union strike.

My dad's consulting career gave him the opportunity to travel the world, where he was able to work as well as indulge his life-long interests in history and geography. His first consulting assignment was in Australia, where he developed a master plan to relieve the traffic congestion in Sydney and other coastal cities, as well as to facilitate movement of wool and meat to the various seaports. Part of the work involved standardizing the railroad system by utilizing the same gauge track in each province. While in Australia, he and Mother attended the 1956 Olympics in Melbourne and witnessed the moving of the damaged Navy ships from the Battle of the Coral Sea – an important battle that saved Australia from being invaded by the Japanese in World War II.

After Australia he worked in Sri Lanka getting tea and rubber over mountains and rough terrain to seaports. In Calcutta, India, he was able to fuse his humanitarian concerns with practical business solutions. He was responsible for finding homes for many of the homeless in his efforts to alleviate traffic caused by workers living in the streets. He solved similar traffic problems in Athens, Greece, and many others. Over the next 10 years he and Mother traveled to 27 countries in six continents. They never made it to Antarctica. Mother's chief duty in all these assignments was to keep them healthy. This involved assuring that all drinking and cooking water was boiled and safe, using local produce and even teaching sanitary techniques in more than one instance. After their world adventures, they established their residence in Hamden, Connecticut.

My active tour of duty with the Navy also came to an end in 1956 as Dwight Eisenhower was elected for his second term as President. For that service I received the National Service Medal. With the experience I had received over the three years, I elected not to return to Westinghouse. Instead, I took a job as manufacturing manager of Madison-Faessler Tool Company in Moberly, Missouri. The company made a variety of proprietary tools for the railroad, truck and automotive industries.

On December 17, 1957, our second son, Robert Thomas, was born. Joan went into labor that night and I was with her in the hospital. About 2:00 am I saw the doctor taking a drink out of a bottle. Being concerned I asked him what it was and he gave me a drink of pineapple juice. It was a long night but well worth the wait. Mother and Dad returned from Australia to visit their new grandson. They brought stuffed Koala bears for Bob and a unique scooter for John.

At this time we acquired our first dog. It was very playful to the extent that when Bob would try to crawl on the floor the dog would grab his diapers and pull him back. Fun for the dog but Bob didn't think much of the game. Even though Joan's life got busier with the second child, she found time to teach science to 6th & 7th grade students at the local elementary school.

Joan and I were both heavily involved in our Presbyterian Church. Joan taught Sunday school and I was a Deacon and President of the Men's organization. We thought it would be interesting to introduce the group to a fundraising chili dinner. It was met with something less than enthusiastic support. One of the members called me over later and said; "we hate chili". It certainly brings home the thought that you need to know your market before introducing new ideas.

In 1958 Madison Industries purchased two additional companies and decided to merge all three into a former mill building in Providence, Rhode Island. I was asked to assume the title of President of Faessler and move the operation from Missouri to Rhode Island. I accepted and went about the daunting task of organizing the move. The plan was that the first trucks loaded would unload at the back of the new facility and the last trucks in the front. For a variety of reasons no truck kept to the schedule. Growing up in the transportation business and working on logistics for the Navy proved invaluable, as we essentially had to start over. Eventually, it all worked out successfully, but it was quite an ordeal.

In the meantime we found a delightful home in the wonderful peninsula community of Barrington, Rhode Island. When I first was assigned to Corpus Christi in the Navy, I started to invest in Merrill Lynch's Monthly Investment Plan. I began with just three stocks and reinvested the dividends. Those investments provided the funds for our purchase of the Barrington home. It is always a good idea to plan for the future and invest wisely.

My parents' travels around the world were both informed by and contributed to our family's values. There was surely a greater appreciation of life in the United States as most of the people they encountered in other countries were not as well off as people in the U.S. My family has always valued the study of history in illuminating who we are – as individuals, as a family, as a country, and now, even as a global people. They were able to share our family's values and also share in others'. As informed by their travels, they became even more convinced by common practical solutions over ones shaped by political or religious dogma. As an example, my father had USAID money to build a plant to convert fishmeal into bread flour. When the plant was completed, the local Buddhist priest objected to the process on religious grounds and would not permit members of his congregation to consume the bread made in this manner. In the meantime, Mother discovered the Indian artist Jamini Roy. He was to become one of the most important Indian painters of the twentieth century. She bought for me his painting "Woman on Horseback". Joan and I thought it would not look good in our house so it hung over my workbench for many years. I sold it at auction in 2007 for five figures!

Jerry & Joan Frieling honeymoon at the Broadmoor Hotel,
Colorado Springs, CO, 1952

Jerry Frieling, U.S. Navy, 1953

Bob, Joan, John, & Jerry Frieling, Barrington, RI, 1959

Gerald Harvey Frieling Jr.

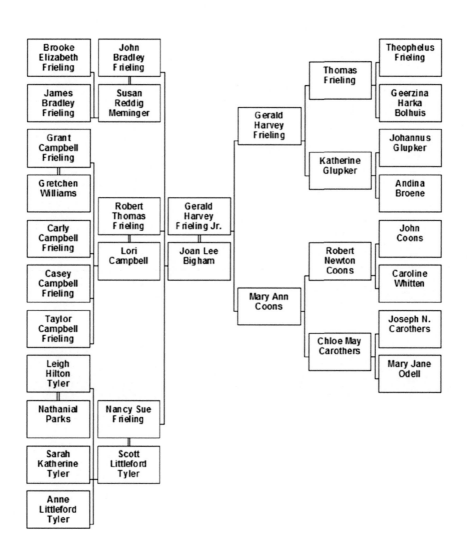

CHAPTER 10

TI & Barrington in the 1960's

At about this time Texas Instruments had acquired the patent for semi-conductors from Bell Telephone Laboratories. TI then bought the Metals & Controls Company in Attleboro, Massachusetts, to give them a materials and component parts capability. Along with their acquisitions, TI began decentralizing the company into strategic business units. I joined TI in 1959 as the operations manager (manufacturing & engineering) of the Precious Metals unit and later became its General Manager when the industrial wire operations were added. It was a great time to be with a growing and technology- based company. My skills and experience matched TI's. I worked with a very dedicated and professional group of people where we set goals to introduce major new products each year. Examples of these were the telephone service cable, copper clad aluminum wire used as the center conductor for coaxial cables (for which I won the Wire Association's medal award), a high strength corrosion resistant cable for underwater use, and a copper wire with glass to metal sealing properties used in electronic applications. During that period, I was granted three patents. I received the Wire Association's Research Award for one of these – the manufacture of metallurgical bonding of clad wire. It definitely was an exciting experience and one where I received my first stock option.

One aspect of the job was that I was able to do some international travel. An early trip took me to Germany where I witnessed first hand the devastation caused by the Second World War. Bunkers were still there, along with bullet holes in buildings, and mounds of rubble from the cleanup. They were just starting to put Cologne back together. Operating out of a sales office in Geneva, Switzerland, and a plant in Bedford, England, the products of the Division were promoted throughout Western Europe. An interesting sidelight was that I had the opportunity to give a speech to the Italian parliament on how to improve that country's balance of payments problem. It was fascinating to walk up the red carpet and into the chamber where the members were waiting, and then to meet several of them afterwards in a reception room. It was frustrating to later learn that few of the recommendations were actually adopted.

When I was back at home, I spent any free time improving our house on Lantern Lane. It had a breezeway between the house and the garage. I decided to enclose it and to make it into a family room. It was a great idea but not without some interesting events. It started when the concrete truck came to pour the floor. I had forgotten to reinforce the framing and as soon as the concrete started to flow the supports buckled. A neighbor offered some excess tile for the floor. Unfortunately, the industrial grade tile was a nightmare to install, particularly the sticky tile cement. Joan and I were covered head to toe in the nasty stuff for days.

At home during the Christmas season we started the tradition of having a children's party. It was generally held in the now completed breezeway, with a buffet dinner served in the dining room. Each parent would drop off a present sometime before the party. During the evening of the party Santa would arrive and present each child with his or her present. One year a small boy kept tugging at Santa's coat asking, "Have you got one for me?" Wouldn't you know his present was the last one out of the bag. It was a great way to usher in the season and has even been duplicated on occasion by our children for the grandchildren's friends. Ironically, the Tyler's in their family have long done the same thing.

It was during this time that Bob, our second son, suffered a tragic accident. He was playing with a group of friends and somehow, a wire that was used to tie up a bundle of newspapers penetrated his right eye. He lost sight in that eye. It was a black day that we all remember often.

Life in the Northeast offered a multitude of outdoor activities in which we participated as often as possible. As John started school, Joan continued the family tradition and became den mother of John's (and later Bob's) Cub Scout troop. The meetings were usually held in our home. Later, as a Boy Scout, John had the opportunity to attend Camp Philmont in Arizona, where he further sharpened his camping skills including how to deal with rattlesnakes on the trail.

We were also introduced to Camp Beckett. Located in the Berkshire Mountains, this YMCA camp was outstanding and provided many years of great camping, teamwork building skills, and outdoor training of all types. John received the 1 in 50 award at Camp Becket for the outstanding camper and subsequently had the pleasure of introducing his son Jay to the camp who attended for several summers and also participated in the International Camper Exchange Program where he spent time in a camp in Sweden and lived with a Russian family for a few days. Bob also introduced his son Grant to the camp and daughter, Carly, went to the girl's sister camp – Chimney Corners.

The boys took swimming and sailing lessons at the Yacht Club. John also participated in Little League baseball and was fortunate to be playing with some other very talented boys. John had good hand-eye coordination and played a mean third base. Bob developed an interest in skiing and became an excellent downhill skier. He even participated in aerial acrobatics. In the winters we would take trips to Waterville Valley, New Hampshire, to both learn and to perfect our skiing ability. These truly were some wonderful family times. In fact, TI used us as an example of how to balance career and family. Interestingly,

Bob uses this legacy in his company today teaching his employees the importance of having balance in their lives.

For three years during this period I also taught in the evening graduate school program of Brown University in Providence, Rhode Island. The course I developed was a management course on how to manage using the profit & loss and cash flow financial statements. It was a very enjoyable course, but because of time commitments both at work and home, I stopped teaching it after the third year.

On July 3, 1963, our daughter Nancy was born. What a joy that was – truly a bang up event. Providence Lying-in Hospital would not let the expectant fathers stay for the birth so when they called I cut some roses from our bushes, put them in a vase with water, and brought them to the hospital. On the ride to the hospital, I proceeded to spill water all over my pants, much to the delight of the nurses. When Nancy and Joan were due to come home from the hospital a few days later, I was not there. My dad provided the transportation as our next-door neighbor and I were in a sailing race. Nancy has never let me forget where I was when she needed to come home from the hospital. We were sailing the Flying Dutchman, which was an Olympic class boat.

It was the summer of 1963 in New England. John F. Kennedy was president and sailing was at its peak. I certainly wanted to participate in the excitement. We had an 18-foot powerboat, which we used for recreation in the waters of Narragansett Bay. Picnics on one of the various islands in the bay, as well as cruising along the coast, made for some enjoyable outings. I also continued racing. In one race, we were caught in the tail of a hurricane. We put the spinnaker pole through the forward ballast and sank the boat up to the bow. Our rescue by the Coast Guard made the front page of the Providence Journal. Leaving from the dock in front of their house in Jacksonville, FL, Julie & Bill Buckingham and their family enjoyed sailing on their Morgan 34.

After Bob and Lori acquired their second home on Cape Cod, Bob purchased a 36' Boston Whaler for cruising and fishing the waters around the Cape.

Later in the year, I was in a staff meeting when one of our associates came in and broke the news: President John F. Kennedy had been assassinated.

The Thanksgiving and Christmas season had always been important time for our families and Joan and I continued the tradition. During the Christmas season we always made it a point to go to New York City, to explore the sights and stores and to see the shows. Nancy in particular both then and years later, really enjoyed the Rockettes at Radio City Music Hall and the Nutcracker ballet. We also made it a point to eat at a really fun or ethnic restaurant.

Between the skiing in New Hampshire, Christmas in New York and two weeks each summer on Cape Cod, we were able to spend quality, and sometimes funny, times together. On a camping trip to New Hampshire I locked the car keys in the trunk. We then spent the next hour convincing Bob to crawl into the dark trunk from the back seat to retrieve the keys. On the same trip, I had brought along a shark sailing boat with a soft plastic hull that would not tack into the wind. We almost did not make it to back to shore after a sail on the lake. When we finally did, being able to recount the stories over the campfire made up for the frustrations and missteps.

My sailing partner was a Canadian who with his wife lived next door to us. One weekend in 1966 we decided to go to Canada for a weekend of skiing. On the second day I hit some snow-covered rocks on a downhill run, which crossed the skis and because the bindings did not release, broke my ankle and leg. I spent the next week in the hospital in St. Jerome and then another two weeks of recovery at home. On the flight back to Boston from Montreal members of the Bruins hockey team would not sit next to me out of superstition. Nancy was a young girl at the time. Joan dressed her in a nurse's uniform and she attended to her "patient" everyday - very cute and a wonderful memory.

Nancy, Bob and John had fun together with their lemonade stands and visiting the spook house on Halloween. It was also enjoyable going to Boston for the Red Sox games. John especially remembers when I was able to get one ticket to the 2nd game of the 1967 World Series between the Red Sox and Cardinals and let him get out of school and ride to the game with some of my work associates. We always attended the 4th of July parade in Bristol, RI, in our Morris Minor convertible. We had many friends. We loved the natural beauty and coastal environment of the area.

TI was a great and exciting place to work. It was the equivalent of working for Apple or Google today. The company was at the cutting edge of technological advances, as well as corporate structure. TI was led by some of the best business executives in the world. I knew many of them personally. The technological and decentralized environment drew talented young people from all over the country to its various locations. In spite of the benefits, two of my life's goals were to become a member of YPO and the CEO of a public company. And so with many mixed emotions I accepted an offer from Air Products and Chemicals in Allentown, Pennsylvania to become a corporate Vice President and President of the Metallurgical Division.

To acquaint us with the Allentown area they provided a subscription to the local newspaper. When the boys asked why we were receiving the paper and I told them, they threw it at me. We moved to Allentown in 1969. This was perhaps the first concrete example of how goals drive decisions.

CHAPTER 11

Air Products & Allentown in the 1970's

Taking the Air Products job was truly a difficult decision. Earlier in life I would not have hesitated, but my family loved our life in Barrington, especially the boys. Eventually, I moved our family to Allentown because of opportunity, both in career advancement and social mobility. In my famous letter to Joan's parents, I laid out my goals, and these truly did shape my life's decisions.

The first thing we noticed when arriving in Allentown was the rolling hills. We took advantage of that and found a wonderful home in Brookhaven, which was near Emmaus, a suburb of Allentown. It was important to us to be within driving distance to New York City so we could continue our Christmas traditions. Nancy would later take the lead in our holiday celebrations. Everyone (family, friends, even acquaintances) remembers Nancy's wonderfully animated Christmas programs that she performed for us. Even on occasion getting the dogs involved. It really set the tone for the season having her stand in the bay window telling us what Christmas is all about.

Nancy entered the first grade, Bob was in his last years in elementary school, and John started high school. John took advantage of the local trout fishery to complete his Eagle Scout requirements that he started in Barrington. In fact we went back to Barrington for John to receive his eagle certificate and badge. I was very proud of John staying with the program as I received my Eagle award about 30 years earlier. Scouting has meant so much to the family for so long. The fish hatchery was important in another incident. Bob entered an 8th grade fishing contest, which was held in the Lehigh River adjacent to the hatchery. He won a $25.00 savings bond for catching the largest fish.

In the first summer after arriving in the Allentown area, John went to Sweden as part of the International program with Camp Becket. He lived with a Swedish family and had the opportunity to acquaint himself with their culture and certain parts of northern Europe. International travels and experiences with other cultures were important to my parents and to Joan and myself, and we wanted to pass on this family trait. As a point of emphasis, during our marriage, Joan and I have visited all 7 continents and traveled to many countries in the Americas, Europe and the Far East. One Christmas, I gave Joan a cruise on the Queen Elizabeth II to the Caribbean. It was the first of several cruises we have taken over the years; a wonderful way to relax and enjoy the Ports-of-Call. A few years later, we took the QE II again - this time across the Atlantic to meet our friends, Norman and Jean Birch from England, on our way to tour the battlefields of Europe. Our children and grandchildren seem to be following in this tradition. For example, Bob and his family have traveled to nine international countries, while John's family has traveled to nearly as many, with their children traveling to even more due to their individual pursuits.

During John's adventures in Europe, he and some friends were supposed to take a train from Stockholm to Frankfort, Germany. After the train left, it separated at a stop when they had gone to the front where the café was located. They ended up separated from their group and arrived on the West Coast of Sweden in the middle of the night. Fortunately they were able to take a hydrofoil across the Baltic Sea to Copenhagen where they met their train and continued on to Germany. Before he left home, his mother did not want him to take the bus to

Allentown from Emmaus, but early exploits on trains is part of growing up a Frieling.

John did very well in high school - both in sports and academically. He excelled in football and basketball. As quarterback of the football team they won the division championship his senior year and he was the leading scorer on the basketball team. It was not without some pain, however. Tackled while running down the sideline, he tore his ACL, which required surgery and several months of recuperative therapy. As a senior he was named scholar-athlete of the year. It was during those years that he met and dated Susan Meminger who was later to become his wife.

The Meminger's have an interesting family background. Susan's father, James S. Meminger, born July 7, 1929 in Lancaster, PA, was a banker in Allentown, was an outstanding tennis player in both high school and college, and was inducted into the Elizabethtown College Sports Hall of Fame. He can trace the family back to the Aargau section of Switzerland in the 1400's. An early Meminger ancestor to enter America was Hans Jacob Hollinger from Boniswil, Switzerland (James' great-grandmother on his father's side was a Hollinger). A farmer from the Swiss/German area, he arrived in the Port of Philadelphia on September 21, 1731, aboard the Ship Brittania with 24 others.

James' mother, Anna Margaret Snyder, was an accomplished pianist and the daughter of the first pharmacist in Lancaster County, PA. He is credited with promoting the control and labeling of over-the-counter medications and became one of the first millionaires in the state.

James' father was Cyrus Hollinger Meminger who served in World War I, after he and the rest of the Franklin & Marshall senior class petitioned the president for early graduation so they could enlist in the army. Cyrus served as an officer in France during the war. His father was Dr. James W. Meminger, a prominent Reformed Church minister in Lancaster, PA. His church grew to be one of the largest east of the Mississippi. He was married to Florence Hollinger, whose father was Amos Hollinger. Amos won a blue ribbon at the Paris Exposition for his English Riding saddles. He is also credited for supplying 13,000 pairs of leather shoes to the Union Army during the Civil War and constructing a large rambling brick home that came to be known as "Hollinger House".

Dr. Meminger was the son of James G. Meminger of Perry County, PA. James G. Meminger, Susan's great-great grandfather was a Civil War hero, who fought and was injured at the Fort Stedman breakout attempt during the Battle of Petersburg, Virginia on March 25, 1865. Shortly before being wounded himself, he wrote a moving letter from the battlefield to the widow of his friend:

To Mrs. Sarah Schull: Your letter of the 18th came to hand, addressed to your husband (Frederick Schull). God help you, my friend, that your husband is no more. We went into battle on the 25th, and your husband fell, pierced by a rebel ball. I was near him when he fell, and I can assure you he suffered no pain. He was shot through the heart, and all he said was, "Oh! I'm killed! He fell, and expired without a struggle or a groan. We have taken care of his body, will have it embalmed, and send it home immediately. Sad news and a sad duty to send it to you, but such is the fate of war.

Your husband has fallen, but it is a consolation to know that he died in the triumph of a Christian faith, and hope in the atoning blood of Christ, his Saviour and Redeemer. He died as brave men love to die-with the Star Spangled Banner waving over him, and the shouts of victory ringing in his ears.

It is our Heavenly Father's will. Do not be cast down. The Lord orders all things well, and if He cares for the sparrow, even, He will care for you. God bless, farewell.

General Robert E. Lee surrendered the Army of Northern Virginia to General U.S. Grant a few weeks later. After the war, James dropped one of the M's in the name in order to make it easier for the farmers in the area to write it. Ironically, another relative was C.G. Memminger, who was the Treasury Secretary of the Confederacy. After the war, he founded both the Public School system and the Memminger School in Charleston, South Carolina. He pioneered integrated education, which at the time was a very difficult task.

Susan's mother, Sara (Sally) Louise Reddig, married Jim on May 23, 1953. They had three daughters - Susan, Louise and Ann. Sally also attended Elizabethtown College and was active in Republican politics while living in the Lehigh Valley and served as an elected delegate for the Republican Party Presidential Conventions three times. Her mother, Elva Grimes, married Horace "Brooks" Reddig who served as a medical clerk in World War II. In fact, at age 36 with a wife and two children, Brooks was the oldest man drafted during World War II from Lancaster County. This was because of the high number of Amish and Mennonites in the area that declared Conscientious Objector status in the county. A draft number of two also put him at the front of the line. The Grimes side of the family remains close, holding annual reunions and sharing recipes. The Grimes Family cookbook is in its third publication. Another unique fact is that Susan's family can claim DAR and Sons of Liberty status from five sources including one woman, Abigail Rice, who served as a nurse at the Yellow Springs Hospital in Chester County, PA. Yellow Springs was the first military hospital built in the United States; it was commissioned by General George Washington.

Susan earned her undergraduate degree and master's at Rider University in Lawrenceville, NJ. She earned her Ph.D. from the University of Pittsburgh and worked for a time at the highly regarded Western Psychiatric Institute in one of the early studies on anxiety. Once Susan and John moved to Boston, Susan was able to join the top clinical psychiatry practice in the country at Mass General Hospital. In addition to her clinical practice, she also published papers on various topics in her field. In one of the groundbreaking studies on the topic she studied five generations of a Boston family to find the "anxiety" gene. That work resulted in her promotion to Assistant of Professor in Psychiatry at Harvard Medical School and MGH. At that time, this was a rare distinction for a woman but not surprising considering the successful women in her lineage, Susan has always said that her connection to the large Grimes' family inspired her to begin the genetic linkage study. In addition to her 25 year career at Mass General, she also taught 3rd year Harvard University medical students a course called Doctor Patient which taught the students how to relate better to their patients. Beginning her career at a time when women were just starting to assume a more active role in the workplace, Susan deserves credit for the professional way she managed her career.

John finished high school at Emmaus and then he enrolled for college at Duke University. At Duke, John joined the Sigma Alpha Epsilon fraternity and was selected to attend its leadership school between his freshman and sophomore year at Northwestern University in 1974. I had also received that honor and attended the school on the campus of Southern California in 1948. On graduating Cum Laude with an AB degree in Economics and Religion from Duke in 1977, John went on to Cornell University School of Law graduating with a J.D. degree in 1980. At graduation he was asked to join the law firm of Reinhart, Boerner, Van Deuren, Norris and Rieselbach in Milwaukee, Wisconsin. He specialized in mergers and acquisitions, leveraged buyouts, and generally all phases of corporate law. He and Susan were married in a wonderful candlelight ceremony in Emmaus, PA on October 17, 1981. Following a honeymoon in Jamaica, they purchased a home in Whitefish Bay, WI where they stayed for the next several years until the migration to Boston. Lori and Bob joined them in Boston later the same year.

Bob's tenure in Allentown was very memorable in many ways. He finished elementary school, and then he started high school playing football as a freshman on the same team as his brother John. His football career was cut short by a back injury during his junior year while competing in the State track championships at Penn State University. However, Bob went on to receive the award for the most varsity letters (12) in his four years at Emmaus High School. He was an outstanding track star in high school where he competed primarily in the triple jump. Not only did he win the school and district championship, with record setting jumps. He also went on to the University of New Hampshire where he set the school record that would last for over twenty years. Over his career Bob set over 20 different track records.

Bob was also into biking. He had a touring bike that took him on trips throughout the surrounding countryside. On one such trip he struck a rock on a fast downhill run and flipped over his bike. He landed hard on the gravel road. A Good Samaritan helped Bob and his broken bike get back home. He broke his collarbone and had lacerations all over his back.

Like John, Bob also had the opportunity to travel to Europe on the Camp Becket International program. He went to Greece and lived with one of the Greek Generals who was in power at that time. Like his brother, he too, had the opportunity to experience the local culture and travel to other locations within Europe. One weekend Bob and some friends from Camp took a boat and sailed around some of the Greek Islands.

They camped out overnight on one island and in the morning, they found out that they were sharing the beach with a nudist group.

Like many before him, on both sides of the family, as a young person Bob was the ultimate entrepreneur. He sold the line of Fuller Brush products door to door and operated, with John, Security Photo, which recorded personal valuables on film for clients who wanted an accurate record for insurance purposes. He stayed with these business ventures through most of his high school years.

We had two golden retrievers during this period. The first, Rusty, was a favorite of Bob's. Rusty had a habit of bringing us chickens, ground hogs, boots and anything else he could find. Rusty was a great dog and it was an extremely sad day when he was killed by a truck on Bob's birthday! We replaced Rusty with Sandy, another Golden Retriever, who stayed with us until the end of the decade.

Winters in Allentown were typical for the Middle Atlantic region with plenty of snow on occasion. One particular night Bob and John decided to take the toboggan to Lehigh County Club and try out the hills. It was almost a disaster when they hit a couple of bumps going too fast. They fell off the sled, were knocked a little goofy, and found the sled down by the river. The Pocono Mountains provided good skiing and we took full advantage, particularly at the Sky Top lodge. It was on the bus back from a school ski trip to Stowe, Vermont that Bob met a delightful young lady named Lori Campbell. Lori in future years would become his wife. Coincidentally, Susan and Lori grew up directly across the street from each other in Emmaus.

Lori's ancestors came from both Italy and Ireland. Her father's great-great grandfather emigrated from Ireland to Waltham, Massachusetts, at the time of the potato famine. Upwards of 2,000,000 Irish left their home country during that period and immigrated to the United States, Canada, and other countries. His son John Ray Jr. became Clerk of Courts in Boston and for many years was the mentor of John McCormack, who became the Speaker of the House of Representatives in the United States Congress. John Ray, Jr. was born in 1897 in Dorchester, MA, and went into the Navy in World War I with all his entire Harvard class. After the war he went into the insurance business with Metropolitan Life where he was part of a team that organized the first group life policy in the United States. Later he was appointed Regional Director of the Social Security system for New England, and before retirement, he established similar systems in Brazil, Greece, Chile and Indonesia. For his work he received the highest award from the Brazilian government. He married Gertrude Cunningham in 1931 in the depth of the depression where they moved to Dedham, MA. John Ray III, Lori's father, was born there in 1935.

Lori's maternal great grandparents were Carolina (born 1882) and Joseph (born 1869) Balboni. They come to America from Cento, Italy settling in Wellesley, Massachusetts. Joseph and his family were gentleman farmers who were recognized for their compassion and caring for those in need. A daughter Mary was born in 1908 and graduated from Wellesley High School as valedictorian. She was an assistant to the President of Wellesley College and honored for her many years of work with the American Red Cross. At age 19 she married Hamlet Collina. All the Collina boys were named after Shakespearean characters because their father loved the opera. Hamlet was born in Bologna, Italy in 1901 and served in the Italian Army in Ethiopia. In his early 20's he came to America and also settled in Wellesley. Hamlet and Mary had a daughter Caroline (born in 1935) who is Lori's mother. Caroline, who graduated college in 1957, was the first in her family to become a college graduate. She married her high school sweetheart, John Ray Campbell III.

Before their marriage John and Caroline were the King and Queen of their senior prom at Wellesley High School. John went onto Rensselaer Polytechnic Institute on a ROTC scholarship. After graduating he became a Navy carrier pilot. He was also selected to enter astronaut training but instead joined Air Products & Chemicals in 1963. John (Buzz) and Caroline moved to Allentown with their daughter, Lori, born 1958, and son John Ray IV, born 1961.

Buzz and Caroline moved 11 times as Lori was growing up so they never lived close to family but as both grandparents lived in Wellesley, MA they travelled there on holidays and summers. It was a memorable time for Lori as she related well to both sides of the family enjoying homemade Italian meals, warmth and love from one and stories with an academic and travel focus from the other. During those times Lori would receive lots of attention especially since they both treated her as a grown-up. As a result of those experiences, conversations and observations, Lori absorbed their values and culture that has served her well in adult life.

Lori and Bob enjoyed their high school years to the fullest. After he graduated from Emmaus High School, Bob and one of his friends took their bikes and travelled around Nova Scotia. They went 100 miles in seven days carrying 100-pound backpacks. This was a great way to spend the summer, eat some great seafood, and mentally unwind before college. In the fall of 1976 Lori enrolled at Northwestern and graduated in 1980. Bob went to the University of New Hampshire where he majored in Business. He also graduated in 1980. After he and Lori were married, Bob obtained his MBA from Indiana University South Bend.

In high school, Lori was concerned about the labor unrest in the Eastern PA school districts. Lori even got involved when she was a high school senior and the teachers went on strike. As a member of student government, she led the student body in bringing suit against the parties to save their senior year in 1976. Bob even testified at the trial. The experience of seeing the students suffer when the teachers' union and the administration were unable to reach practical and reasonable solutions had a profound effect upon her.

When we arrived from Barrington, Nancy was enrolled in the Emmaus school system as a first grader. Her pleasing personality allowed her to integrate fully in the Emmaus school system and she made many friends. She then transferred to Moravian Academy in Bethlehem, PA for the seventh through ninth grades in order to benefit from smaller classroom size and focused study. Nancy made some wonderful friends at Moravian. Even though it was more academically challenging at first, she integrated well and even became an accomplished field hockey player. During her first year in the upper school, ninth grade, she scored the second highest number of goals.

Since John and Bob had wonderful experiences at Camp Becket, we thought Nancy would enjoy the experience as well so we sent her to Camp Oneka, a girl's camp in the Pocono Mountains. She hated it and could not wait to get home. Bob jokingly sent her a card while she was there at camp that read, "Dear Nancy, we moved," although in retrospect, the card was a portent of things to come.

Nancy, taking after numerous men and women in the family, was as competitive as her brothers. Even the card games, "hearts" in particular, were legendary in their competitiveness. This trait led to her success in numerous sports, especially tennis. Tennis was gaining in popularity and our family took up the sport in a big way. The children began to play and Joan and I frequented the courts at Lehigh Country Club and joined a tennis/dinner group of friends. We also played paddle, or platform, tennis in the winter in addition to the recreation tennis in the summer. Nancy became a very proficient tennis player in high school and later in college and as a participant in city tournaments. In one particular Club singles match Nancy was far ahead and asked her mother, who was watching, if she should let her opponent have a game. Joan and Nancy came to a mutual decision - definitely not. At Ohio Wesleyan University Nancy played varsity tennis for four years and was captain of the team.

In 1977 we celebrated our 25th wedding anniversary by taking John, Bob and Nancy to the Broadmoor Resort Hotel in Colorado Springs, CO where we spent our honeymoon. It had grown from one dining room to nine. From there we took a multiple day raft trip down the Green river riding the rapids. We then drove to Jackson Hole, Wyoming, and Yellowstone National Park. It was a wonderful experience for everyone and certainly one that the children will not forget, especially since I was the only one who brought a pillow on the raft trip. The next year, we invited my parents and their brothers and sisters to our home for a long weekend celebrating Mary Ann and Jerry's 50th wedding anniversary. This was a very important time for our family to renew friendships and to introduce the children to some of the family whom they had not previously had an opportunity to meet.

The work experience at Air Products was very stimulating and satisfying. The company had acquired Arcair, a welding industry firm located in Lancaster, Ohio, shortly before I arrived. It was made part of my division and was a complement to our other welding products. We manufactured and sold the products through a company network of distributors and to original equipment manufacturers. It was during this time that America won the so-called space race with the Russians and put a man on the moon. Thinking this might represent an opportunity I called the Vice President of Development for one of the prime contractors and asked if they had developed any technology that could be commercialized. The result was that we formed a 50/50 joint venture called Tektran, an acronym for technology transfer, and used several of the patents assigned to the venture to create new products. One was an integrated welding and testing system used to make 2-piece axel housings for the automotive industry. Those systems are still in use. The same technology was used to manufacture the tubular section for cruise missiles. In a separate transaction we acquired the rights to a dashboard alert system that indicated when service or an oil change was required in trucks and automobiles. We installed the unit on most Toyotas coming into the country from Japan. It was the forerunner of today's information system in the instrument panel.

The position at Air Products enabled me to accomplish one of my life-long goals, which was to become a member of the Young President's Organization. I first became a member of the Philadelphia chapter and later helped organize the Northeast Pennsylvania chapter and became its first Chairman. I served on a committee appointed by the Secretary of Army, who was also a member of YPO, to draft the guideline that would be used to replace the draft with an all-volunteer Army. Thirty of our 31 recommendations were accepted and used to draft congressional legislation. My position also allowed me to cooperate with the CIA in doing some undercover work in Russia during the cold war.

In the Allentown community Joan and I were able to increase our philanthropic efforts. I was active in the Chamber of Commerce, Chairman of the $800,000 Building Campaign for the Salvation Army, and a director of Kutztown College. In my work with the Chamber of Commerce, we sought not only to serve existing members, but also to serve the greater community through economic development. Joan was an active member in the Junior League and the Historical Society, at the new Allentown-Sacred Heart Hospital, and at the local public television station channel 39.

In 1979 I was presented with the opportunity to join the National-Standard Company in Niles, Michigan as its President and Chief

Executive Officer. National-Standard was a public company listed on the New York Stock Exchange. If I accepted their offer, I would accomplish my second career goal, but I would have to relocate the family again. Just as John and Bob were not happy moving from Barrington, Nancy was devastated at the prospect of leaving the Allentown area. She had never been to Michigan and with the scenes of the "Blizzard of 78" showing on television and in the newspapers, her vision of moving to Niles was akin to moving to Alaska. It was going to be a difficult transition.

Nancy, John, Bob, Jerry, & Joan Frieling, Lehigh River, Allentown, PA, 1977

Nancy Frieling, 1980

Jim Meminger, Jay & Brooke Frieling, Sally Meminger

CHAPTER *12*

National-Standard and Niles, Michigan in the 1980's

Taking the Air Products job and moving the family from Barrington to Allentown was a challenge but it would also be a challenge moving from Allentown to Niles, Michigan. The task of moving was made more challenging by becoming President of a public company – National Standard. Again, the move was shaped by my career goals and greater opportunities for the family and although there would be a period of adjustment and transition, the move was made for all the right reasons.

I arrived in Niles, Michigan, and started my career with National-Standard in the first week of April 1979. It was actually April 3rd because the current Chairman did not want me to start on April Fools Day. Joan stayed in Allentown until the end of the school year; she and Nancy arrived in June. I had found the perfect house with white columns in front (it looked very much like a fraternity house) located on the St. Joseph River. An odd coincidence was that several of the rooms had the identical wallpaper and paint color of our house in Brookhaven. The house turned out to be located across the river from the site of old Fort St. Joseph, which was a trading post from the mid 1600's to 1781.

In 1980 John was in his last year of law school at Cornell. Bob was a senior at the University of New Hampshire and Nancy was just starting in High School. New schools, jobs, friends, and marriages were all to be a part of the decade of the 80's.

In 1984, both sons and their wives decided for different reasons to move to Boston.

During his time practicing law in Milwaukee, John was fortunate to have joined a firm that was very business oriented and, unusual for a lawyer, he was able to participate in not only legal, but business discussions with clients. During his time doing leveraged buyouts, he was able to learn the business aspects of buying and selling companies. One such deal was a management led leverage buyout of a division from Allis Chalmers, a Pennsylvania defense contractor located in York, PA called Precision Components Company. John always thought that both the management and business were excellent and he made a point of staying in touch with them in case there were opportunities in the future. After a while, John decided that he wanted to get into the business side of deal making. At the same time and having just completed her Ph.D., Susan also thought her opportunities were better on the East Coast. They had a chance to go back to either Pittsburgh or Boston. Having fond memories of growing up in Rhode Island and spending so much time in New England, John and Susan decided that they would go to Boston.

Ultimately, John joined Bariston Associates, which was a boutique investment banking and private equity firm, and stayed for 10 years as a principal until he began his own firm called Deerfield Partners. During that time, John completed many successful and interesting transactions, but was always on the lookout to purchase a company. As it turns out, his friends at PCC had a subsidiary that they were looking to sell called DC Fabricators and John together with other investors, bought the company in 1999. DCF is a defense contractor designing and manufacturing condensers for nuclear submarines. Since John's involvement, it has grown 150% in sales. Five years later, he also bought PCC. This company had some challenges at the time and John needed to do some creative financing and negotiating, particularly with the Pension Benefit Guaranty Corporation, to navigate through a solution that had never been done before. As a result of this and other actions, John was able to manage the company through these various challenges so well that its revenue has grown over 400% since he first became involved. John recently merged the two companies together and serves as its Chairman and principal stockholder.

In addition, John and Susan have taken on an immense challenge in helping The Skating Club of Boston build a new three-rink facility in Boston. John is managing the overall project and Susan is instrumental in organizing the trophies and other memorabilia that will be prominently displayed in the new facility. If completed, this $80 million development will be one of the finest in the country.

On graduating from college Bob took a management training position with an industrial products company in Mishawaka, Indiana and lived at home. It was a good position to have as the country was entering a period of economic recession and Bob's job was reasonably secure. On August 16, 1980, he and Lori were married at Chagrin Falls, Ohio, where her parents were currently living. It was a wonderful ceremony, which was thoroughly enjoyed by everyone. After the honeymoon in Northern Michigan, they found an apartment in South Bend, IN, and shortly afterwards, they moved into a house in one of the South Bend neighborhoods. After several years Bob knew that he would be much happier in a company with a stronger entrepreneurial culture. So Bob came to Boston and slept on the couch in Susan and John's apartment for a month looking for a job. As a consequence he found his career with Northwestern Mutual Insurance Company and together with Lori moved to Boston in 1984. The company had a vibrant financial planning practice, which Bob represented as part of the Boston agency. He later became the managing partner, one of the youngest in company history. He moved the agency to Wellesley, MA in 1994. It has become one of the top performing business units of the Northwestern system, and he now has five offices in Rhode Island and Massachusetts. To raise awareness among his coworkers for community service, Bob and Lori founded the Wellesley Group Charitable Foundation. This non-profit organization raises money in support of various charitable activities in the area. Examples include care packages for service men and women, Children's Floating Hospital, and several children's cancer programs including funding a 5-year old girl's dream of visiting Disney World in Orlando, FL as part of the Make-A-Wish program.

At National Standard I was elected to the Board of Directors and became President and Chief Executive officer of the company. National-Standard with annual sales of over $300 million, had a long history in the wire business producing both wire and machinery used in the tire industry. They were also leaders in the production of welding, spring and communication wire, with plants located in the United States and various international countries. One of the first major problems that awaited me was over-diversification. It was during the 1960's and early 70's when diversification was a popular growth model that the company purchased several companies that did not relate well to the core business or have any appreciable market share. As a result I divested 17 operations over the next several years. Another problem was that the country was in a period of high interest rates with the subsequent effect on the value of the dollar. This opened the U.S. markets to greatly expanded international competition. The results of this are still in evidence today with lower prices, outsourcing and the decline of middle management jobs.

During this period I was asked to join the board of directors of several public and private companies. Among those were CTS, Elkhart, IN; Tokheim in Fort Wayne, IN; Brockway Glass in Brockway, PA and Jacksonville, FL; Hunter Foundation, Niles, MI; Protection Mutual Insurance, Park Ridge, IL; First National Bank of Niles, MI and a regional advisory board member of Liberty Mutual Insurance in Itaska,

IL and the University of Kansas School of Engineering. Although most of the boards only met once a quarter, it greatly expanded my network of business executive acquaintances. This provided an insight to operational best practices that other organizations were using that could be applied at National-Standard. An interesting event happened at CTS during my tenure when they were subject to an unfriendly takeover attempt. In the process of defending the action I was called as the company witness at trial in the Second District Court of Appeals in Chicago. We lost that round but went on to win the case in the Supreme Court. We thereby protected the control share statute, an important takeover defense for all public companies. I joined the board of CTS in 1982 and served continuously for the next 27 years becoming the longest serving director in the company's history.

Nancy's first days at high school were an adventure trying to find her way around. One day when looking for the cafeteria she ended up in the boiler room. During her high school years Nancy continued her success at tennis and along with Bob, also honed her skills in skiing. Between her junior and senior year she went with the Students Abroad group playing tennis and skiing in all the countries around the Swiss Alps. It was a tremendous experience. She proved to be popular in school and met Scott Tyler, a very nice student athlete excelling in football and wrestling. On the Students Abroad trip, Nancy wrote a very poignant letter to us thanking her mother and me for giving her the opportunity to have the international experience and also that she was developing an interest in Scott Tyler beyond being just a friend.

The Tyler family was originally from England, but immigrated to the United States where Leon Tyler, Scott's grandfather, became a respected educator in Michigan. As an entrepreneur, Jerry Tyler, Leon's son, started Tyler Refrigeration in about 1927, which manufactured and sold cooling display cases to retail grocery stores. The business flourished under Jerry until his untimely death along with his wife and son, in a Chicago hotel fire in June 1946. Bob Tyler, Jerry's brother and Leon's son, who was working in the company at the time, became president and operated in that capacity until it was acquired in 1963 by Clark Equipment, a large industrial equipment manufacturer with headquarters in Buchanan, Michigan. Taylor (Tim) Tyler, Bob's son and Scott's father, was in the business after graduating from Dartmouth but left to start an automotive dealership selling General Motors products. Tim married Marjorie (Midge) Stegeman in November 1960.

The Stegemans were originally from Bremen, Germany and immigrated to this country in the mid-1880's. Midge's parents Jane and Robert Stegeman settled in Fort Thomas, Kentucky, where Midge was raised. Midge's mother originally was a Littleford, whose family was from Shropshire, England. The Littleford family immigrated to the United States in the late 1700's and settled in the Baltimore and Cincinnati area. Another relative, William H. Donaldson, originated Billboard Magazine in 1894. The Stegemans prospered in the machine tool business. Tim and Midge settled in Niles, MI after they were married. They had four children, the second oldest of which was Scott, born November 2, 1963.

One summer I had Scott and a friend working on the terrace that ran from our backyard to the river. We had planted it with fruit trees, scrubs, and flowers. As they were digging and weeding, they had great fun finding turnips and throwing them into the river. The turnips were tulip bulbs!

After graduating from high school Nancy continued her studies and tennis at Ohio Wesleyan University. She played varsity tennis for all four years and was captain of the team her senior year. Scott went to Denison University playing quarterback in a single wing formation on the football team was captain of the team in his senior year and was president of Beta Theta Pi fraternity. Nancy was a Kappa Kappa Gamma and since the schools were not that far apart they had some great times together. On graduating Nancy was offered a position with

100

an advertising firm with an office in Hilton Head, South Carolina. She accepted and earned valuable experience in advertising while enjoying some beautiful weather. Scott accepted an offer from Procter & Gamble and spent the year in Milwaukee, WI.

On July 11, 1987, they were married at the Presbyterian Church in Niles, with the reception being held at the Signal Point Club. It was a great event with many friends and relatives attending. After the ceremony and a honeymoon in Barbados, Nancy and Scott established their home in Milwaukee, only to move back to Niles a few years later where Scott joined his father in the automotive dealership.

On January 25, 1986 our first grandchild was born - Grant Campbell Frieling. It was truly a celebration as we were having a Chicago Bears Super Bowl party. We had a cake commemorating both events. Grant grew up in Wayland, MA, where he excelled in academics and athletics. He participated in state championship teams in both soccer and track. He went on to the University of Notre Dame, graduating cum laude in 2008 but not before passing my class in corporate strategy. During his four years in college we had the opportunity to have many on-campus lunches together, in addition to having his classmates and friends to the house for dinner.

In November 2010 he married Gretchen Williams from St. Petersburg, Florida, who was in her final years of medical residency at the Harvard Medical School in Boston. They are a terrific couple, who now reside in Brookline, MA. On August 3, 2014 Gretchen gave birth to our first great grandchild, Madison Elizabeth Frieling. Grant currently is a district manager in Bob's insurance agency and Gretchen is completing a pathology fellowship at the University of Vermont.

Our second grandchild was Brooke Elizabeth Frieling, born November 10, 1986 in Boston, MA to John and Susan. Brooke became a very accomplished dancer and ice skater who arrived at the skating rink at 5:00 am for her training during all four years of high school. After graduating from high school, she moved to San Diego, CA where she made the jump from a Novice to Senior competitor, an almost unheard of advancement. Later she was asked to train with top-level world coaches in Philadelphia, PA who subsequently found her a partner with which to compete. They developed into one of the top ice dancing teams in the world, competing throughout the United States and Europe in over 12 international competitions, which culminated in their participation in the 2011 World Skating Championships held in Moscow, Russia in which they were ranked in the top 20 in the ice dancing competition. In her early years she was in the intensive track at Boston Ballet and performed in approximately 100 performances of The Nutcracker at the Wang Center in Boston, participating for several years in various roles. She is a graduate of the University of Pennsylvania in 2014 with a major in Communications from the top ranked Annenburg School of Communications. Brooke will continue to pursue her interest in dance and performing at Florida State University where she was granted a scholarship to pursue a Masters degree in Fine Arts in Dance.

We had two grandchildren born in 1988. Carly Campbell Frieling on October 24th and Leigh Hilton Tyler on November 28th. Carly graduated with a degree in psychology from Boston College and is putting it to good use in a recruiting role for a college internship program with Northwestern Mutual. Carly has been an anchor in their family offering steady support to Grant and Casey as they dealt with type 1 diabetes. In grade and high school Carly excelled as an athlete and school leader; playing lacrosse, soccer, running track and participating both on the student and class council. She also demonstrated talent as a tap and hip hop dancer. She began her college career at Trinity College in Hartford, CT and then transferred to Boston College during the middle of her sophomore year. She was a key defender at Boston College on their club lacrosse team where she earned the title of "the beast" because of her speed and strength on the field. She continues to be an anchor and strong, steady influence in the family as they deal with various medical and life issues. Carly provided volunteer assistance for Homeless Children making a positive difference in the lives she touched. In the near future she hopes to train and run in the Boston Marathon.

Leigh was the first child of Scott and Nancy. She graduated from Niles High School where she played basketball and participated in all kinds of school activities including the National Honor Society – an honor that her two sisters also enjoyed. It was where she met her future husband, Nathanial Parks. As a young girl Leigh enjoyed learning to cook and bake on her "Little Tykes Kitchen".

When Leigh was in the first grade I was still serving on the University of Kansas School of Engineering advisory board. The School, in collaboration with Southern Methodist University and the Smithsonian Institute, had developed a science program for elementary schools. With their permission, I brought the program to Niles, and with the consent and encouragement of the School Superintendent introduced it to Leigh's first grade class. For the balance of the school year I taught the program for an hour each Monday morning. Leigh suggested I call myself Mr. Science and so for the class and their parents I was forever known by that title. The program was a success witnessed by their higher test scores on the mandatory Michigan State science achievement test the students take in the fifth grade. At the end of the school year, a regular science teacher took over the program teaching it for many years.

After graduating from high school, Leigh enrolled at Syracuse University. Even though the school was not a perfect fit she enjoyed the nutrition classes as they rekindled her passion for baking. After her freshman year she transferred to Michigan State University where she graduated in 2011. Following graduation, she attended the French Pastry School in Chicago and received her certification as a pastry chef.

Leigh and Nate were married on August 3, 2013 in a beautiful ceremony followed by a honeymoon in Hawaii. Leigh continues her love for baking as a free-lance pastry chef. Nate also graduated from MSU the same year majoring in business. He accepted employment with Plante-Moran, a public accounting firm in Lansing, MI earning his CPA with the firm. In 2014 he left P-M to become associated with the administration department of MSU utilizing his accounting background.

For the first time, in 1985, I visited our operations in South Africa. I later returned to visit Tokheim's operations. In total our personal and business travel has taken me to all seven continents. Also in 1985, Chloe May Coons died September 4th in a retirement facility in Branson, Missouri just 29 days before her 107th birthday. She fell in the shower, broke her hip, contracted pneumonia in the hospital and passed away. The moral for all elderly people is, *don't fall!* In 1986 the space ship Challenger exploded not long after lift off. All on board, including the high school teacher Christa McAuliffe, were killed. I was attending a board meeting of Brockway Glass in Jacksonville, Florida, that day and from the top floor of the bank building, saw the tragedy unfold.

My employment agreement with National-Standard stipulated that I could retire at age 60. After 10 years as Chief Executive and in discussion with the Board of Directors, I elected to take that option and pursue other interests, including teaching. At the beginning of 1990 I was presented with the opportunity to teach an MBA course in corporate strategy at the University of Notre Dame. Thus, I began another interesting chapter in my life.

Jerry Frieling, Susan Meminger, John Frieling, & Joan Frieling, 1981

Lori Campbell & Bob Frieling Wedding, 1980

Nancy Frieling & Scott Tyler Wedding, 1987

Lori, Grant, & Bob Frieling, 1986

Susan, Brooke, & John Frieling, 1986

Scott, Leigh, & Nancy Tyler, 1988

Taylor (Tim) & Marjorie (Midge) Tyler

Caroline and John (Buzz) Campbell – 2014

Nathan & Leigh Parks, Nancy, Anne, Sarah, Scott Tyler - 2013

CHAPTER 13
Tokheim and Notre Dame in the 1990's

In addition to being offered the opportunity at Notre Dame I continued to be a director of Tokheim, a manufacturer of gasoline pumps about the same size as National Standard and CTS. The board of Tokheim felt at this time that the company needed new leadership and offered me the position of Chairman and Chief Executive. I was flattered, but as I had made the decision to retire, I told the board that I would accept the offer on an interim basis until a new Chief Executive could be recruited and hired. This process took longer than I had anticipated so throughout the decade of the 90's I served the company in various capacities as Chief Executive, Chairman and finally as Vice Chairman of the board.

It was a fairly exciting time. We started as the third largest supplier of service station gasoline pumps in the world and after making several acquisitions secured our position as number one with annual sales approximating $700 million. Two of the acquisitions were European companies, which again meant overseas travel. Most of the time Joan did not accompany me on international business travel. However, in 1991, the board of CTS wanted to visit their operations in Asia. As Joan had never been to that area of the world, I suggested she meet me in Hong Kong. We then traveled to Japan and saw the country by rail pass where we ate and slept in traditional Japanese style. It was a wonderful way to experience their culture and see the people up close and personal. One of the most moving experiences was visiting the nuclear bomb memorials.

To balance out the requirements of teaching and business I leased an apartment in Fort Wayne, IN, which was the headquarters of Tokheim. I would drive there after class on Monday morning and return either Thursday or Friday depending on teaching, business and personal requirements. This lasted until 1995 when we hired a new CEO, but I continued as non-executive Chairman. In 1998 we passed the Chairman's title to the new CEO and I became Vice Chairman until the company was sold to Dresser Industries, later Halliburton, at the end of 1999. It was also during this time when I decided to join the International Senior Amateur Golf Society and play in tournaments around the world. One took us to New Zealand and Australia in 1997. I continued playing with this group for the next ten years. My uncle, Robert Sidney, was also an avid golfer playing well into his 80's and winning the Missouri Seniors Championship several times.

The decade of the 90's saw the rest of our nine grandchildren born; Sarah in 1991, Jay in 1992, Casey in 1992, Anne in 1993 and Taylor in 1996. All of them have played a great role in all our lives, and we are fortunate to have such a wonderful and talented group of young people around us. It is such a pleasure to watch all of them grow up and mature before our eyes.

Sarah was born March 7, 1991 in Niles, MI. As a young girl Sarah always had a passion for art. For many birthdays and Christmases her favorite present would be art supplies. From high school she went to Miami University in Oxford, Ohio where she majored in art education with a minor in psychology. Upon graduating in 2013, doing practice teaching in the field, she realized that she wanted to get her master's degree in art therapy. She has been accepted to pursue that degree at the Art Institute in Chicago starting in the fall of 2014. Earlier, Sarah had a strong interest in horses. She was thrown during a show with the horse landing on top of her and causing her to lose consciousness. In the spirit of "getting back on the horse", Sarah still loves to ride whenever she can. In high school she excelled in soccer, being awarded all-district honors her junior year, and like the other girls had many extracurricular activities. Late in the season her junior year she tore her ACL in a soccer match but made a complete recovery playing again her senior year and winning a $500 soccer scholarship for her outstanding play and overcoming the adverse effect of her injury. In one of her first year art classes at Miami she had the assignment to build a frame complete with canvass and then creating a painting on it. On a break from school, Sarah came to the house with the materials and we made the 3' x 4' frame and stretched the canvass over it. She then painted a strawberry shortcake which, in our opinion, was a masterpiece. It now hangs, on loan, in our kitchen. Thoughtful, talented and compassionate Sarah will make a wonderful art therapist and teacher.

Jay was born in Wellesley, MA on January 11, 1992. He was and is a very kind person interested in the welfare of others having many friends demonstrating responsibility and leadership in all their activities. A few days after his 8th grade graduation, he was complaining of a pain in his head and ultimately had trouble walking. Rushed to the emergency room, he was diagnosed with a brain abscess. An emergency craniotomy was performed at Mass General, which required more than a year to recover his strength and return to normal. Susan's medical experience was key in preventing a misdiagnosis and perhaps even saving his life by insisting they perform a CAT scan first before operating.

As a result, Jay was unable to participate in sports in high school. Feeling healthy again by his junior year, he "wanted a challenge". The solution was to join the Massachusetts National Guard. During the summers following both his junior and senior years, he went to Basic Training and Advanced Individual Training at Fort Benning, GA. While there they found out that he was an "expert" marksman. Weeks after starting college at the University of Rhode Island, he was notified that he was being deployed to Afghanistan as part of Operation Enduring Freedom. At just over 19 years of age he was the youngest deployed by the Guard since WWII. Jay served with distinction as a combat infantry soldier in Nangarhar Province completing 80 missions as a "first dismount" gunner and driver his convoy once being hit by an IED. Declining the opportunity to come home early because he was "committed to the full deployment" his duties increased due to a reduction in force coming home finally in April 2012. No doubt it was a maturing and character building experience and we are all proud of his service. As a result of his time in Afghanistan, Jay earned the Army's Commendation and Good Conduct Medals in addition to the Afghanistan Campaign and Global War on Terrorism Metals. Jay is now continuing his college at University of Massachusetts-Amherst majoring in Political Science. As an illustration of Jay's kindness and compassion he noticed a homeless man on a very cold day in Amherst. Instead of giving him money he went to a store and bought the man a warm hat and gloves.

Casey was born on June 10, 1992 Wayland, MA and attended both grade and high school there. She supported the high school and its sports teams by becoming a varsity cheerleader, was captain of the squad and is in addition a fantastic dancer. After graduating she enrolled in the nursing program, a course of study in which she has always had a high degree of interest, at Northeastern University in Boston. She is currently in her last year of a 5-year work-study program in which she will receive both classroom and practical in-hospital training. She has particularly enjoyed the action and excitement of the emergency room. Casey is considering a PhD in nursing to teach or become a nurse practitioner. She has had medical challenges in her life including Type 1 diabetes but also endometriosis and lots of food allergies however she is strong with an amazing sense of humor, which has helped in overcoming some of these adversities. She likes yoga and painting and her goal is to merge eastern and western medicine for the good of her future patients. She testified before Congress at the age of 14 in an effort to bring awareness for the need to fund diabetes research. In high school, like Carly, she volunteered at Horizon's for Homeless Children and was a sparkle in their lives.

Grant was diagnosed with juvenile diabetes in 1998 followed by Casey in 2004. At that time Bob & Lori's family became very involved in the diabetes world. They participated in the Walk-to-Cure Diabetes by creating "Team Cure", which raised over $2 Million for diabetes research over 10 years. It was a huge effort that involved 350 community members and transporting them to Boston to walk 5K in support of the 13 families dealing with Type 1 diabetes in the Wayland area. Over that 10-year period they received the distinction of being the top fund raising team in the country. For six years during this time Bob was a director of the Juvenile Diabetes Research Foundation.

Anne was born September 3, 1993 in Niles, MI. She is a very compassionate and competitive person. Anne excelled in high school sports especially cross-country running and soccer being named to the all district team each of her four years. As a senior she won the Joseph Whitwom Sportsmanship Award given to the athlete who best embodies the spirit of sportsmanship. When Anne was a junior in Niles high school, as part of her service requirement for the National Honor Society, she tutored a third grade class and loved it. She had discovered her passion for teaching young children. As a result, she is now at Purdue University studying to be a primary education teacher. In the summer after graduating from high school, Anne and I put on a magic show for the members at Signal Point Club in Niles. She has a natural stage presence and the show was a huge success so much so that many of the members are still talking about it. As an avocation, Anne loves to sing. She put that talent on display at Leigh and Nate's wedding when she sang a beautiful solo.

Taylor was born September 12, 1996 in Wayland, MA. She is a good all-around athlete playing both basketball and lacrosse in high school and captain of the lacrosse squad in both her junior and senior years. In addition Taylor plays defender on one of the State club lacrosse teams spending many hours on the field in practice and competition. She has been recruited to play lacrosse at Union College where she hopes to attend in 2015. In keeping with the family traditions, Taylor has spent her high school summers doing community service camps working with the women's shelter in Boston and interning with high school students who are severely physically and emotionally challenged. Her life goal is to be a guidance counselor in a high school to help teenagers make their way into society. She is also an outstanding dancer and hopes to pursue that in some way in college. Taylor has a beautiful signing voice and would like to find time to develop that further as well.

It is interesting that all the grandchildren have found their career passions and are pursuing their dreams to accomplish their goals. Of equal importance is the generosity and time commitment that each of the families are doing in the service of others. Susan and John by donating their time and talent to the Skating Club of Boston's effort in building a new facility; Bob and Lori in their commitment to "Rosie's Place", a women's homeless shelter, work on the Public School Foundation and support for the Business School at the University of New Hampshire; and Nancy as a board member of Ronald McDonald House Charities, the Niles-Buchanan YMCA, the Lakeland Hospital Health Foundation and as Treasurer of "Hope Grows", a cancer support organization.

In 1997 three acres of property on the river and close to our current house became available in Niles. We purchased the house and land and began to plan for a new home. After tearing down the old house we spent the next two and a half years where we planned, designed and built our dream house for the future. It turned out to be magnificent. We moved in on Thanksgiving 1999 and have enjoyed the property ever since. We included an apartment above the garage where most of the grandchildren stay during their visits. We took time out in 1998 to visit Antarctica on the "Little Red Ship". It was a fantastic adventure. The ship sunk a few years later when it hit an underwater iceberg.

During the 90's, my involvement with Tokheim decreased as my teaching load at Notre Dame increased. I started out teaching only corporate strategy in the MBA program and judging case competition. I was then able to offer the strategy course to undergraduate seniors. This added a whole new dimension, as undergraduates do not have the advantage of work experience and tend to be less vocal in class. I thoroughly enjoyed the students, however, and was appreciative to the University for giving me the opportunity to share my experiences with them. We began having each class over to the house for dinner once each semester and this provided a great venue to get to know them on a different level. Teaching at the University of Notre Dame was a very rewarding experience. Notre Dame was the culmination of the college-level teaching I had done off and on throughout my business career.

Finished Niles home - 1999

Jerry Frieling, Gretchen Williams, Grant Frieling, & Joan Frieling, 2010

Leigh Tyler & Nathan Parks - 2013

CHAPTER 14

Niles 2000 and beyond

The new millennium did not start out well. Joan was diagnosed with uterine cancer, which necessitated an operation coupled with postop radiation and chemotherapy. She, of course, lost her hair but throughout the process kept her spirits high and ultimately triumphed.

Beginning in 2000, I was able to again expand my teaching involvement with the University of Notre Dame. In addition to corporate strategy, I taught Leadership, Business Planning & Entrepreneurship, Supply Chain Management, and Not-For-Profit Administration. At times I felt like the utility infielder, but I enjoyed the variety and the different mix of students. Each of the courses was for only undergraduate seniors or graduate students.

In 2003 after returning from a golf tournament in Mexico I was diagnosed with coronary heart disease, which required open-heart surgery to unblock and to replace five arteries to the heart.

Joan had her left hip replaced in 2006 and followed with her right knee in 2007. She had gallstones and her gall bladder removed in 2010, which contributed to being hospitalized with C-Diff soon afterwards. In 2011 Joan was diagnosed with pancreatic cancer. She underwent a "Whipple" operation that resulted in 54 days hospitalization.

We have just proved that a high percentage of your total medical bills and experiences occur later in life. Currently Joan is cancer free and both of us are enjoying each other's company. We were also able to celebrate the marriage of two of our grandchildren. As previously mentioned, Grant married Gretchen Williams a medical doctor from St. Petersburg, Florida, in 2010 and in 2013, Leigh married Nathanial Parks a CPA that she had known since the fourth grade. They are two delightful couples, and their weddings provided opportunities for the whole family to be together.

In 2010 John and Bob (together with Jay and Grant) provided an extraordinary 80th birthday celebration by arranging a fly-fishing trip to Montana. In addition to fishing, we were able to go white water rafting and tour Yellowstone National Park. It was truly a memorable experience.

To put the time period in perspective, the first Gulf War was in 1991 with the Iraqi War starting in 2003 and presumably ending in 2013 or 2014. The conflict in Afghanistan started in 2001 and in 2014 was winding down. Barak Obama has two more years of his second term as President of the United States.

In a paper written by Nancy for a college assignment, she noted that her parents and her brothers were her main role models, and influenced her in profound ways. They all stressed the importance of a strong work ethic and the value of a good education to further one's career and life. They also provided a level of confidence when the road ahead was uncertain and difficult. The fact that they are involved with outside activities proved to her that even though they are successful in their careers, they found time to contribute to the broader community. She expressed that she was proud that she had seen their ambition and dedication carry over to other members of the family. After reading her paper, we were delighted that she understood the family values and were proud that she embraced the values that had been passed down in our family for so long.

50th Wedding Anniversary of Joan and Jerry Frieling,
Family on-board ship to Bermuda, 2002

CHAPTER *15*

Culture and Family Values

As mentioned in the introduction, this book is an attempt to answer my mother's question of whether the children had learned the cultural values of the family. As best as I was able, I traced the family's history as it shaped and was shaped by these values. As the family's story becomes more complete, the difficult task of codifying the family cultural values becomes more imperforated as well. Some of our family's core values are shared by most families, such as the importance of actually spending time with family. Some values are common among families such as the importance of hard work, but are manifested differently in our family through the emphasis on goal setting. Some of our family's values have been important from however early we can trace our family, such as generosity. Some other values may have originated in other countries but took on important American modifications throughout the generations.

Strong Family Ties and Faith Traditions

As you read the history of our family the one over-riding trait that should be apparent is the strong family tie culture. As mentioned earlier in the book, Frank Allen always emphasized to his children the importance of family background and character. Not only do the family members like and respect one another but they are there for support, encouragement and advice whenever needed. Of course our immediate family spent vacations and holidays together as I've described many of the trips Joan and I took with our children, but there has been a strong emphasis on getting the extended families together as often as possible.

As best symbolized by the farmhouse that Mary Jane built, our strong family tie tradition has included the notion of "home" as a place not only of great comfort but as a place one is always welcome to return. When Joan and I built our Niles home, we made sure we had plenty of space for visiting children and grandchildren and even great-grand-children. Though it isn't Mary Jane's farmhouse, we used the idea of her house and welcoming spirit as a model for what we wanted to build.

The importance of the extended family unit is perhaps best illustrat-ed by the extended family meeting grounds, which was the summer-house on the dunes of Lake Michigan. Being the oldest grandchild of Thomas and Kate by ten years, I was often the lone child milling about the lake house with Aunt Grace, my parents and grandparents, Uncle Arthur (and later, Aunt Hazel), Uncle Ted (and later, Aunt Ollie). These early childhood experiences of the closeness of the extended family shaped many of the ways I viewed my own children and their spouses and families and my grandchildren and their spouses and families. I remember sitting on the back porch of the Lake house with the "guys" as they enjoyed a warm beer with Thomas. In the Dutch tradition granddad always kept a case of beer outside – never in the refrigera-tor. Because of the closeness of my parents and their siblings, I saw how important the acceptance of suitor and potential spouses was to them. I also saw how difficult earning acceptance could be, but once a new member was accepted into the family, the acceptance was total.

A significant factor for the strong family ties has been a system of shared values, which is, in a sense, the reason for this chapter. These have produced a set of behavioral norms, which have established im-plicit boundaries in terms of standards of acceptable behavior. Mary Ann described it as not discipline per se or rigid explicit rules but norms, which defined the boundaries including such things as dress, manners, ethics and interpersonal conduct. These have defined the identity of the family over the years. Although it might at first sound contradictory, adhering to the non-rigid but accepted norms encouraged individual expression within these family norms.

One of the shared values that exemplifies the strong family ties is the family's faith and its expression during the holidays. The family faith is central to our story, and it goes back to when the family split its name over the Protestant/Catholic division at the time of the Reformation. The faith traditions of the family have been mostly on the Protestant side and mostly in the Reformed brand of Protestantism, but our family has grown to include Catholics and Protestants of all denominations.

Even though the faith journey has been central to the family from the beginning, it was most often expressed in the American versions of Dutch Reformed with its Michigan roots and the American form of Presbyterianism with its congregational and Puritan roots. Dr. James W. Meminger was a prominent Reformed Church minister in Lancaster, PA, and Harke Frieling was a pastor in the Dutch Reformed Church in numerous states. I also noted that Mary Jane and Chloe May hosted various church functions at their house, and the way in which other family members, along with Joan and myself, have been involved in church activities.

Our family faith has certainly shaped the shared values examined in this chapter. It has shaped the strong emphasis we place on the family unit, and even the importance of work as a spiritual enterprise. The important concept of a compassionate God has certainly shaped our philanthropic efforts. One of the primary ways our faith has manifested itself is through our holiday celebrations.

Mary Jane and Chloe May's holiday celebrations were just that, a celebration of faith and family. From the incredible homemade food to the homemade gifts, their celebrations set the standard for generations to come. Joan and I have always attempted to continue the traditions.

When we lived in New England we started an annual pilgrimage to New York, where both Nancy and the boys enjoyed the sights and sounds. We, in part, chose the location of our home in Allentown to be within driving distance of New York City so we could continue these holiday excursions. We, also, began the tradition of having a children's Christmas party complete with buffet dinner and a visit from Santa. Nancy's Christmas programs became well known and she would later take the lead in the family holiday celebrations. Many of these traditions have continued with our children and grandchildren, along with new ones of their own.

What has been consistent is that the family members have respected their legacy. They have taken the family's shared cultural legacy and adapted the central principles for each generation. No one could have embodied this better than our daughter Nancy when she wrote to us from her dorm room at Ohio Wesleyan University on November 7, 1983: "...we were talking about our families and it hit me that my family does care and everything is important and it's these things that are not taken for granted. I want you to know I feel lucky and fortunate to have the kind of family togetherness we have...but I'll tell you that when you live with people from different backgrounds your own family is the best".

Value of Hard Work

It goes without saying that hard work is an accepted value in the United States and countries throughout the world. This has been especially true in the Reformed religious traditions that have been dominant in our family since the Protestant Reformation. From the very beginning of the Frieling name, mentioned in Chapter one, our family's success and even its survival are owed to hard work. Our family has epitomized the Protestant Work Ethic. This has manifested itself in two unique ways: the full embrace of the entrepreneurial spirit together with embracing the free market system, and the belief and practice of setting goals.

Examples of this are found throughout the book from William Odell, who believed he would not receive his fair share, to Bob, John and Scott who left large corporations in favor of smaller entrepreneurial enterprises. Mary Jane and Chloe were forced to make their own way, especially with the death of Mary Jane's husband, Joseph, when Chloe was seven. Not only did Mary Jane manage the household and three children, she managed the farm and the family business. Chloe May, my grandmother, developed this independent spirit early and it remained intact until she died a short time before her 107th birthday. Whenever I would call her, the first thing she would ask me is what I thought of the government's farm policies. She and many others in the family did not like the waste she saw as silos full of corn were left to rot or pigs were slaughtered to artificially control prices. A person worked hard, invested wisely, and tried to create a competitive advantage, largely through education. The entrepreneurial spirit had served them well and has been passed down in the family.

Our family has always been goal driven and it is easy to see how this legacy has influenced my personal and professional life. When Bill returned to the farm after graduating from the University of Missouri, he established goals for growing the dairy business. Frank Allen Bigham, a goal setter, was successful in many business ventures. I, also, am an example of how goals drive decisions. As set forth in a letter to my future in-laws, I had two goals; one was to become a member of the Young Presidents Organization and the second was to be the CEO of a NYSE listed public company. The pursuit of these goals shaped major life decisions. When I was teaching at the University of Notre Dame, I would have many students ask me for advice. I always responded by saying you have to have meaningful goals in your life that you strive to achieve.

Value of Education
The value our family has placed on education is evident throughout the book, as I have detailed the impressive educational background

of our children and their spouses and their children. The family's belief in the value of education goes back to the immigration of William Odell and his wife Rebecca to America. They were some of the first Puritan settlers and part of the Massachusetts Bay Colony, who were known for their emphasis on education, and where formal education in the United States began. In 1635 the early Massachusetts settlers created the Roxbury Latin School and in 1636 founded Harvard University. The first printing press arrived in 1638 and shortly afterwards they were writing books for children and discussing ideas on how to eliminate the difficulties of communicating with them. In 1642 the Massachusetts Act was passed which required that all children learn to read. Our family shares history with another early Ivy League school. The Honorable and Reverend Johnathan Odell was a medical doctor who graduated from the College of New Jersey (now Princeton University) and served as a surgeon in the British Army.

The story of great-great grandfather Andrew Jackson Odell cutting notches in the trees so his daughter Mary Jane could find her way to and from school has resonated in the family for years. I can clearly remember my grandmother, Chloe May Coons, talking to my mother and myself, on just about every occasion possible, about the importance of education and using that story as an illustration of the dedication necessary to achieve it. Chloe's husband, Robert, was known for his book collection and interest in a wide range of subjects.

My father was the only graduate of a four-year college in his family up to the time I was born. On my mother's side, only Bill Carothers and Robert Coons went to college. Joan's family was much the same. Her mother and uncle had degrees but no one else. That is not surprising given the agrarian and immigrant background of the families. However, education was very important to all of them and they emphasized it to their children. This educational priority can be seen in the education of the women in our family, usually much earlier than was common in the United States.

Education has been important to our family in the fullest sense of the word. This includes classroom education, social activities, and athletics. From Bill starring in football for Missouri a century ago to the recent success of Brooke in ice dancing and Taylor in lacrosse, a consistent theme throughout the family has been the tradition of athletics and travel. As mentioned in previous chapters both have been important to the values and stories, which have been part of the family's legacy and legends. One example is that Scott and Leigh Tyler, as 10-year olds swimming for the Niles, MI, YMCA on the "10 & under" relay teams, both broke the pool record, marks that stood for many years until the building was retired from service. As first the father, and then 25 years later, the daughter achieved a record that will not be duplicated.

It does not matter whether male or female, travel and athletics have been an important part of the family for generations. At this time, the family's travel award goes to Joan's cousin, Bill Altaffer. He holds the world record for visiting the most UNESCO World Heritage sites (892 of 936), as well as being the third most-traveled person in the world. He's visited all 192 UN countries, plus 300 island groups, exhausted 14 passports and 130 visas. He currently lives with his family in San Diego, CA.

Teaching has been a lasting part of the family legacy. My aunt Ollie wrote a textbook and was a teacher in the Detroit school system. Frank Jr. and Harriet were teachers. Joan taught school at various times in her life. I taught at various colleges along the way including the graduate school at Del Mar College in Corpus Christi, the graduate program at Brown University, and undergraduate and graduate students at the University of Notre Dame. Recently, our granddaughters, Sarah and

Anne are both pursuing career goals in education. Whether we have taught full time or part time or even as volunteers, teaching has been a way for us to share our experiences and give back to society.

American Values

As with many immigrant families, our cultural legacy was shaped by the journey to and settling in a new land. As the genesis of the family, for the most part, is Western Europe, we have carried with us those European values and transplanted them into the great open spaces of America, which presented a vast array of resources and seemingly unlimited opportunity. However, integrating different cultures and legacies is no small task as culture is the totality of learned socially transmitted behavior, ideas, values and customs of people living in a common society. The common unifying force of achieving this integration is law.

Our family has always had great respect for the law and the Constitution and the Bill of Rights upon which the laws are based. Respect for the law then is a positive action meaning that it is an act of affirmation. Respect for the law is not merely not doing something negative but is doing something positive by behaving in such a way that a person acts affirmatively to manifest a respect for the law and helps it to evolve. This action is fundamental to creating an orderly and just civilization as well as a positive functioning family unit.

Consistent with respect for the law is the fact that America was founded on the principle of individual rights. In America no ideal is held higher than the concept of everyone being an individual with the freedom to be who you are without constraints. This is embodied in the Declaration of Independence by stating that the individual is endowed with certain unalienable rights, among these are Life, Liberty and the Pursuit of Happiness. It follows then that individuals will form a commonwealth or government to protect these rights.

As our family is the integration of many European cultures it is easy to see the impact of respect for the individual as we molded various values and beliefs into a way of life that resulted in business and personal success. Honesty and integrity have been paramount in our interpersonal relations. It has been important to respect differences of opinion, an individual's personal space, and do nothing verbally or physically to harm another person. The family has always valued the study of history in illuminating who we are – as individuals, as a family, and as a country. As a result, and as previously alluded to in light of my parents' travels around the world, the family has favored common practical solutions over ones shaped by political or religious dogma.

As individuals each of us is empowered to respect one another as individuals, which has become the hallmark of American culture and an important family value. It follows then that respect for property is derived from a learned respect for the individual. From our family's perspective, the idea of personal property took root with the inception of the Magna Carta in 1215 by King John of England in which property rights of all free men in the country were ensured, and the King was prohibited from depriving those rights except through due process of law. In fact, one of the main reasons Mother's ancestors came to America was their dispute with King James I over property that was rightfully theirs.

Taking this idea to America the government's recognition of people's property rights can be found in the 4th and 5th amendments to the constitution. The Fourth Amendment highlights "...the right of people to be secure in their persons, houses, papers and effects, against unreasonable searches and seizures...". The Fifth Amendment extended the concept of personal property even further by saying that no person shall be deprived of "...life, liberty or property without due process of law; nor shall private property be taken for public use, without just compensation." These are important because they define the legal basis of the government's respect for the property of others. Within the Ten Commandments we learn "you shall not steal" and "you shall not covet your neighbors house." In 1862 the Homestead Act was passed allowing land ownership based on the amount of improvements made to the land. This Act helped teach our ancestors to respect other's property; the same value we cherish today. Additionally, intellectual property is protected by various copyright and patent laws which are both exceedingly valuable in protecting trade internationally and over the Internet. Interestingly even I hold three patents.

Perhaps the most important and enduring American value that drew our ancestors to this country was the belief in Democracy. Democracy as a form of government probably began around the fifth or sixth century BC by the Greeks. The word itself is a combination of two Greek words; "demos" meaning the people and "kratos" meaning rule. These two words joined together mean literally "rule by the people". The definition has over time been broadened to include government by the peoples elected representatives and to encompass the principles of social equality and respect for the individual within a community. We have discussed previously the signing of the Magna Carta in 1215, which limited the power of the King or nobles giving some power to the people. These laws were further strengthened in 1628 with the signing of the Petition of Right, which stated that the king could not tax people without the permission of Parliament and in 1689 the Bill of Rights was established to provide freedom of speech and banning cruel and unusual punishment. America took a big step in formalizing democracy as our form of government when in 1776 Thomas Jefferson wrote the Declaration of Independence. Stemming from the Revolution was the system of checks and balances, which mean both the separation of power and the separation between national, state and local levels of government. The separation of power was actually further defined within the context of the French Revolution in 1789 when it was declared that this form of government would be most successful in serving the people if it were separated into three branches; legislative, judicial and executive. As a statement to its success by the 1950's almost every independent country in the world had adopted some form of democratic style of government with the United States being the premier model. Today our democratic government affects every part of our society. One particular important role of government is in education where our young people must be properly prepared to take on the roles and responsibilities in the future and this includes those within government and the political arena. The United States of America was founded on the principles of democracy and now that belief in democracy is instilled in every aspect of our society both domestically and internationally. Its effect can be seen in law, education, social justice, and the corporate boardroom. It may not be perfect but as Winston Churchill said, "it's the least bad form of government around today." Our family has held democracy as the highest ideal, and we have spoken out and served our country to protect this value.

Generosity
Related to all the other family cultural values is generosity. Reflecting our compassion and our belief in a compassionate God (in many forms), our emphasis on education, our democratic values, and even our entrepreneurial spirit, generosity represents one of the most widely shared values in the United States.

In addition to providing a code of conduct, religion has had a significant impact on generosity. It is a central teaching of many religions, emphasizing the virtues of unselfishness and sacrificial giving and not limited to friends and family but extended to those in need within the broader community. Today religious and faith-based organizations comprise the largest category in the non-profit sector, command the largest portion of donations given for charitable purposes and engage the largest number of volunteers. Religious members are more likely to give and volunteer for both religious and secular purposes than those people who do not have a religious affiliation. A faith and belief in God provides both a spiritual and physical need that contributes to an individual's wellbeing and a positive cultural force within the family.

Most of us in the family have had an instinctive compassion toward people and a willingness to help those in need and less fortunate. To understand the importance of generosity and to what extent it exists within the family and United States culture in general we need to look at how philanthropy and generosity towards other people evolved. From the foundation of our country and even in the colonies, generosity was a part of society. It existed both in the form of pure kindness towards others and as a means of increasing the economic welfare of the community in which we were living.

Generosity was an essential part of life for our ancestors, especially those who first immigrated to America and those from a rural background. Like many immigrants, Theophilus Frieling saw America and its values as generous, especially when compared with his own situation in Holland. When he was forced to leave Chicago after the Great Fire, he sought the comfort and generosity of the Dutch community in Michigan. This might not even be considered generosity as it was just an accepted practice, but this would become generosity as it was passed on to future generations.

The same principles applied to Mother's side of the family living in an agrarian based society. When a neighbor was in need the community helped out. That was just the way it was. When a road needed to be built, Mary Jane organized the community, everyone pitched in, and they built the road. It was a practical solution that benefitted everyone; it wasn't generous in that sense. As mentioned throughout the book, practicality and common sense have always been favored in seeking solutions. What once was accepted as necessary and practical became a cultural legacy as it was passed to future generations.

Many examples of generosity can be found throughout the family, from philanthropic donations to investing in businesses where capital is not available from other sources. Without detailing all the philanthropic causes and charities our family has been in position to help, I would like to highlight our family's dedication to the health care field. One of the most important ways our family has contributed to the country's health care system is through our contributions to, working for, and serving on the boards of hospitals.

An early family interest in health care started with Joe Carothers ministering to the sick in Excelsior Springs, then serving in the Medical Corp during the First World War and finally nursing the refuges after the war. Abigail Rice, a relative of Susan's, served as a nurse at the Yellow Springs Hospital (the first military hospital built in the United States at the time of the Revolutionary War). Susan's clinical work and research in genetics and anxiety at Massachusetts General Hospital has been previously documented in the book. Frank Allen, Joan's father, facilitated the building of the community hospital on the family farm and converting the farmhouse into the nurse's quarters. Joan has been an active hospital volunteer both in Allentown and Niles. Nancy is on the hospital auxiliary board in Niles and heads up the "Tree of Love" the fund raising project each Christmas recognizing loved ones. A project originally started by Scott's mother, Midge Tyler. In addition, she is involved in the "Hope Grows" cancer program and is on the hospital oriented Ronald McDonald House Charities board. Cousin Julie's husband, Bill, is an orthopedic surgeon, her son, Brendhan, an Associate Professor of Emergency Medicine at the University of Alabama Hospital in Birmingham and the Medical Director of Highlands Hospital. His wife, Susie, is a practicing pediatrician with the Birmingham Department of Health. Her mother is also a pediatrician and her father is a nuclear cardiologist. Julie has been Director of Development (and past Board President) of Planned Parenthood of Northeast Florida and has been recognized for her efforts in providing quality sex education to teens. She has also been involved in a long time project to provide medical training and equipment to underserved regions of the former Soviet Union and to increase access to preventative oral health care to cities in Russia. Grant's wife, Gretchen, completed her medical residency at the Harvard Medical School, has passed her board exams and is now doing a year's fellowship at the University of Vermont. Gretchen's father, Larry Williams, is a vascular surgeon. Casey is in nursing school and Nate Parks mother, Brenda, is herself a nurse. Lori, as part of her Doula work provides labor and delivery coaching for teen moms. I served for many years on the Memorial Hospital Foundation board in South Bend, IN ending my tenure as Chairman.

To fulfill the American Dream human capital must be developed. This is accomplished by investing in people, and by providing health care, food, and housing as without these little progress would be made. Further, investing in support for education through scholarships, mentoring and training is important for the overall improvement of society and the development of new technologies. We must also invest in justice to help motivate people to expand their capabilities to the fullest providing them with the potential to work, earn, create and produce for their own well-being and that for society in general. There are many ways to accomplish these goals by contributing to the church of your choice, non-profit institutions like the Red Cross or Salvation Army, schools at various levels, becoming an "Angel" investor and many, many others. The contribution that son John is making to the Skating Club of Boston is an excellent example of how an individual can make multiple gifts of time and talent for the benefit of many. Overall, generosity provides a certain amount of psychic income, helps maintain our economy and enhances our reputation in the world. It is clear that the generosity of the American people has become an important cultural legacy in the country and the family and will remain so long into the future.

Epilogue

A consistent message throughout this book has been the importance of the parents on the lives of their children. Parents are the conduit through which culture and family values are taught and explained. I am very proud of the accomplishments and achievements of each succeeding generation. That has been possible by the interest, love, dedication and respect the parents have given to their children. Good parents like good managers are teachers. By word and example values, discipline, goals, initiative and citizenship have been taught by each level of parent or parents in our family. They all deserve our thanks and respect.

On October 18, 2013 at the Freedom Village Retirement Center in Holland, Michigan Mary Ann (Coons) Frieling died at the age of 108 from medical complications following a fall that fractured two bones in her left hip and one in her pelvis. Fortunately she died only two days after the fall, as she would not have walked again. At her funeral she was remembered for her biscuits, oatmeal raisin cookies and a life that was full, complete and compassionate.

In everyday living she believed in self-discipline, a schedule with priorities and before the term was popular, proper nutrition and exercise. At Freedom she always wanted to be the first one up in the morning and have her shower by 7:00am no matter what else was happening that day. She also remade her bed every morning after the staff had completed the task. "They've just not been trained to make a bed right." In the practical sense she knew that things would not always go as planned or turn out they way you wanted. Her words were like the saying goes, "Life is not sitting and waiting for the storm to pass but learning how to dance in the rain." As a father she wanted me to be sure that by word and deed I let the children know that I loved their Mother and that whatever the circumstance the two of us will be there for them. As a parting comment I can hear her say, "...be optimistic with a sense of humor and always remember to be a gentleman."

I believe that I can now honestly say that "yes, Mother, I believe the family is living the values that have been taught and articulated so well by you and others. She had high ideals and expectations for the family but lovingly embraced each and every one of the family members. May God bless you!

To paraphrase an early Greek philosopher "as long as we remember our ancestors the deeds they have done and the values they created they will live in our hearts forever".

About the Author

Gerald H. Frieling, Jr., known to his friends and co-workers as "Jerry" and to his grandchildren as "Pops," has had an interesting career spanning some 60 years. During that time, he has been an innovative engineer, a successful business executive, a passionate teacher, and a dedicated family man. He lives with his wife, Joan, to whom he has been married over the entire course of his career. They live in Niles, Michigan.

Jerry Frieling

15443041R00086

Made in the USA
Middletown, DE
05 November 2014